ME MAKE MONSTER!

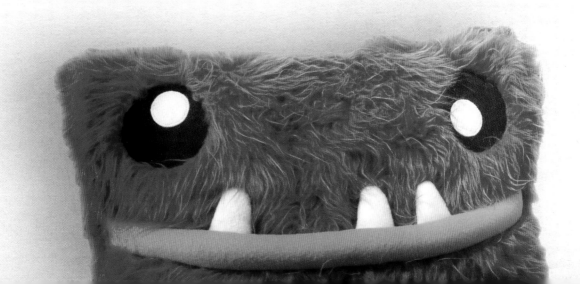

ME MAKE MONSTER!

A MISH MASH OF MONSTERCRAFT

JENNY HARADA

NORTH LIGHT BOOKS

Cincinnati, Ohio

14   13   12   11   10   5   4   3   2   1

DISTRIBUTED IN CANADA BY FRASER DIRECT
100 Armstrong Avenue
Georgetown, ON, Canada L7G 5S4
Tel: (905) 877-4411

DISTRIBUTED IN THE U.K. AND EUROPE BY DAVID & CHARLES
Brunel House, Newton Abbot, Devon, TQ12 4PU, England
Tel: (+44) 1626 323200, Fax: (+44) 1626 323319
Email: postmaster@davidandcharles.co.uk

DISTRIBUTED IN AUSTRALIA BY CAPRICORN LINK
P.O. Box 704, S. Windsor NSW, 2756 Australia
Tel: (02) 4577-3555

Library of Congress Cataloging in Publication Data
Harada, Jenny
  Me make monster! : a mish mash of monstercraft / Jenny Harada. – 1st ed.
      p. cm.
  Includes index.
  ISBN-13: 978-1-60061-863-5 (pbk. : alk. paper)
  ISBN-10: 1-60061-863-4 (pbk. : alk. paper)
  1. Handicraft. 2. Monsters in art. I. Title.
  TT157.H334 2010
  745.5–dc22   2010015019

fw
media
www.fwmedia.com

A MONSTROUS SPECIAL THANKS

Donna's Gourmet Cookies — Donna & Leah Phelps

lilmonster photography

Kids Are Fun Daycare Center — Mema & Meredith

Gregasaurus

EDITED BY LIZ CASLER

DESIGNED BY GEOFF RAKER

PRODUCTION COORDINATED BY GREG NOCK

PHOTOGRAPHY BY CORRIE SCHAFFELD, GEOFF RAKER
AND RIC DELIATONI

PHOTO STYLING BY LAUREN EMMERLING

Metric Conversion Chart

To convert	to	multiply by
Inches	Centimeters	2.54
Centimeters	Inches	0.4
Feet	Centimeters	30.5
Centimeters	Feet	0.03
Yards	Meters	0.9
Meters	Yards	1.1

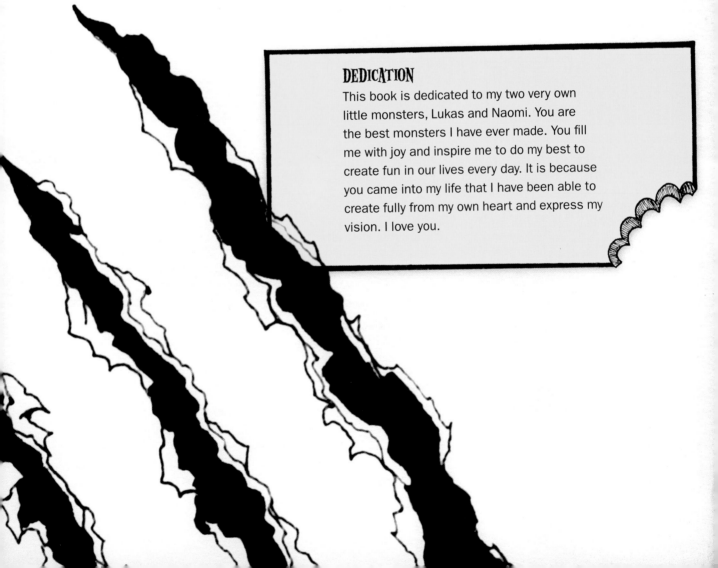

ABOUT THE AUTHOR

Jenny Harada is a lifelong maker of things—she comes from a family of artists and makers. Her earliest memory of the love of creation is learning to sew from her mother at the age of seven. Even then, Jenny always wanted to devise her own techniques for doing things. Her husband, Mark, is a fantastic tattoo artist. They have two beautiful young children and a stinky doggy, and they all live together in New Jersey in a place where the walls are becoming more and more colorful the longer they live there. Jenny attended the Fashion Institute of Technology to study toy design and graphic design, and she has appeared on television demonstrating her crafts. Her work has been displayed in many galleries across the world. She has contributed craft projects to numerous publications, and this is her first full-length book.

ACKNOWLEDGMENTS

I would like to thank my family for sticking with me through the long adventure of writing this book. All the encouragement and babysitting help will never be forgotten. To my loving husband, Mark, and to Oma, Opa and Bubbie: Thank you so much for wading through the ocean of furry, fuzzy scraps we had to cross for me to make this book. Jennifer, I could not have finished without your support and help. Thank you for being there, cheering me on and lending your scissor hands. Margot, thank you kindly for throwing my name into the wind at the precise trajectory. To Liz, my stoic editor—your patience is epic and thoroughly appreciated, and you have been an ever-helpful guide and a fine scout.

DEDICATION

This book is dedicated to my two very own little monsters, Lukas and Naomi. You are the best monsters I have ever made. You fill me with joy and inspire me to do my best to create fun in our lives every day. It is because you came into my life that I have been able to create fully from my own heart and express my vision. I love you.

CATALOGUE OF MONSTERS

INTRODUCTION

Do you see faces in everything—faces with big googly eyes and sharp teeth? I do. I see them everywhere. They are all around me. With every breath I take, monsters jump out at me. As I fall asleep, they emerge from the shadows of my room and then seep into my mind as I teeter on the edge of dreamland. Mostly, they are harmless; but, occasionally, they are actually scary. They are colorful and silly and lovable and weird.

One of my favorite things to do is bring these monsters to life so other people can experience them, too. I love playing around with different materials and tools, discovering techniques, and then combining those materials and techniques. That is how the monsters in this book have come to be. The creatures most dear to my heart are made from fun fur and stuffed with fluffy fluff, but I strongly believe in monster equality, so get ready to play with hard, soft, big and small monster projects.

As much fun as it is to make a monster, the very best thing to do with a monster once it is complete is to give it away to someone you love. Especially if it's huggable. Then you have accomplished three great things in one roaring swoop:

1. You've made someone happy because they know you were thinking of them.

2. You've shared your inspiration, and that ought to give you pride enough for a good howl.

3. You've made room to make more monsters, both in your imagination and on your craft table.

Now, if you want to keep your fabulous new scary (or not-so-scary) friend, that's OK by me, but please watch your toes. There's a very good chance it might be a nibbler.

A HISTORY OF MONSTERS

As it turns out, monsters keep very meticulous records when it comes to their ancestry. How else would they know that fourth-cousin-twice-removed Hildegarde Barumph was the one who introduced the huge mutated incisors into the gene pool, or that it was Great Uncle Barnabus Facklecack who was the first to have those famous Facklecack freckles? Monsters are very serious about keeping track of mutations and dominant traits because by keeping a proper family tree, they can predict which monster babies will have the most awesome combinations of scary features. The Colossal Gigantohuggah has kept particularly interesting notes on his family, which has helped me build a history of monsters.

Once upon a time, before monsterdom became so clever, there were only sea monsters. They were huge and truly frightful. I don't even want to talk about how scary they were. They were bigger than ships, and this is well documented in human literature. We will never know what the sea monsters were thinking by being so ferocious, because those times were before monsters had developed their own written language. There is, however, one individual behemoth serpent that is still alive after all these years, and if you can find him, perhaps he will share with you tales of when sea monsters were the only monsters and reigned the seas. I discovered him once on a scuba-diving trip in the Caribbean. When I tried to get him to reveal the chronicles of old, he became quite furious, and I nearly didn't escape with my life. If it

weren't for my friendship with Gigantohuggah, and the stuffed Basic Beastie I offered him, I surely would have been eaten.

"Aww, did you make this yourself?" he asked and then thrust me away to the surface. Why did he get so angry? Perhaps he is bitter that the glory days of sea monsters have long passed. His distant cousin Gigantohuggah, after all, resembles them in nothing but colossalness.

Another branch of the monster family tree contains a very unfortunate brood of beasts. Each family member had very little in the way of scary traits and possessed much cuteness, which is very undesirable. (Gigantohuggah inherits his fluffy, furry huggableness from these relatives.) It was from this lineage that all monsters in the closet descended. You see, by hiding in the closet where others could not see them, they could maintain a fearful front in the imaginations of human children.

Eventually, from monsters in the closet evolved monsters under the bed. Sometimes monsters in the closet and monsters under the bed can be found living in the same home, but it is rare.

I present this book as the next chapter in monster history. Please know that the monsters you will see here are only a small sample of those that exist in real life. It is up to your own imagination to help create the next generation. Where will the evolutionary roulette wheel land next—on creepy or cute?

CHAPTER 1
MONSTER PELT PROJECTS

You might think no self-respecting monster would be caught dead wearing the likes of rickrack or fun fur, but don't be misled by the poofy, innocuous nature of the materials used to construct the monsters in this chapter. Their snuggly-wuggliness belies their inherent fierceness and generally crabby disposition.

In fact, if anything, all this softy-softy stuff gives these monsters a bit of an inferiority complex, making them prone to lashing out unpredictably—even by monster standards. So, as you're working on them, keep close count of your fingers, toes and noses. Do not tempt them with dangly earrings. And, above all, NO BARRY MANILOW MUSIC! That'll really work them into a frenzy. I don't even want to think about it.

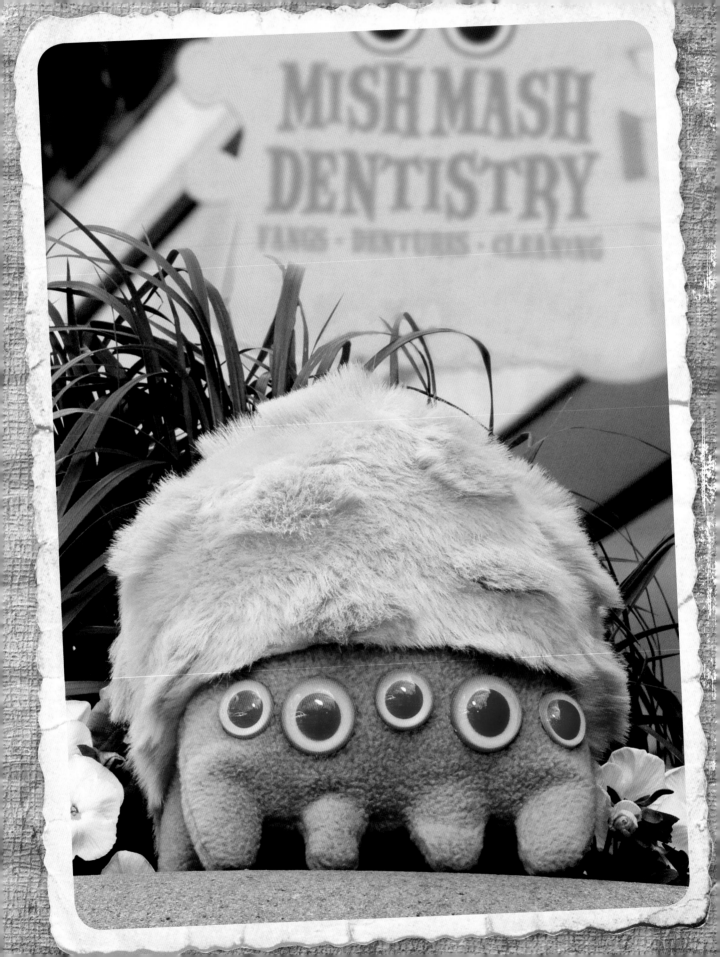

basic BEASTIE

materials & tools

The most basic of all beasties, this one has some very typical monster features. For example, she has five eyes and eight legs, which is a perfect eye-to-leg ratio for monsters. She also sports a fuzzy head that is way too big for her body. Typical. She is very proud to be a model of beasthood. Just don't mention the fact that she doesn't have any big scary teeth—she does not need to be reminded. She is a very confident little beastie until the teeth issue is raised, and then her eight little legs scurry her fast away to hide in the closet.

Pencil or fabric marker

Scissors

18" × 24" (46cm × 61cm) fun fur

17" × 10" (43cm × 25cm) fleece

Sewing machine (optional)

Sewing needle

Matching thread

Pins

5 safety-lock eyes

Polyester fiberfill stuffing

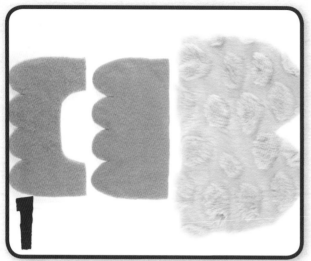

1

You'll need two of each of the feet pieces and two of the head. Enlarge the templates on page 22 and then trace them lightly with a pencil or fabric marker onto the wrong sides of the fabric. Cut out your fabric pieces.

Enlarge the templates on page 22

Monster Tip

When cutting fur, try to cut just the woven backing rather than the fur itself. I use a cylindrical hairbrush to brush the hair out of the way—making a "part" in the fur. Then I cut with the very tip of the scissors so I can be careful about snipping the fewest hairs possible.

2

Sew the two *A* feet pieces right sides together along the inner *U*-shaped cutout. Leave a ¼" (6mm) seam allowance here and throughout. These two pieces will create the space between the two rows of the monster's feet and the inner halves of the feet themselves.

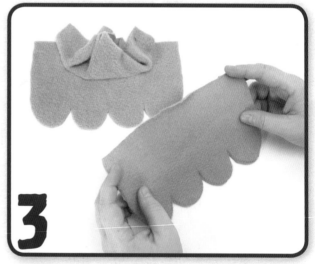

3

Fold one of the *A* feet pieces and out of the way, as shown, to make room for the first *B* foot piece. (Scrunch the folded feet piece as far away from the outer edges as possible so you won't catch its edges in either the pinning or sewing process.) Lay the first *B* foot piece on a flat surface, right side up, and position the *A* feet pieces on top. They will be layered from bottom to top as follows: *B* foot piece, flat *A* foot piece, scrunched *A* foot piece. Pin the *B* foot piece and the flat *A* foot piece together around the edges.

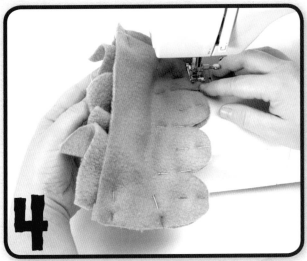

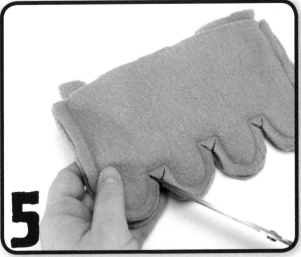

4 Flip over the entire assembly, and sew around the sides and feet, continuing to leave the top open. This can be a bit tricky, so add more pins if you need to. Make sure the edges remain properly aligned, and continue to hold the scrunched pieces out of the way.

5 Notch between the monster's feet with the very tips of your scissors, being careful not to cut the sewn seam. The notches will make it easier to turn the piece right side out.

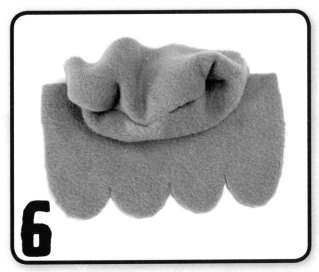

6 Scrunch the *B* foot piece and *A* foot piece that are now sewn together up and out of the way as you did for the *A* foot piece in Step 3. Lay the second *B* foot piece right side up on a flat surface and position the unscrunched *A* foot piece on top. Pin the *A* foot piece to the *B* foot piece.

7 Sew on the final B foot piece around the sides and feet, continuing to leave the top open.

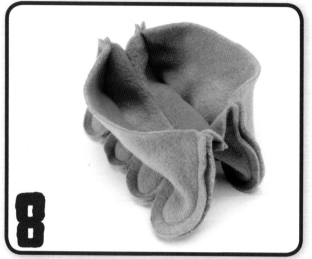

Here is the bottom half of the *Basic Beastie* all sewn together. Leave her inside out for now. Notch between the set of feet you just sewed as you did the first set in Step 5.

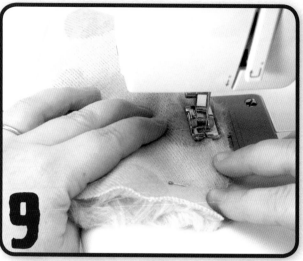

Fold each head piece in half, right sides together, so you're looking at a single, pointed dome. Pin and sew the dart marked on the template. (When pinning fur, tuck the strands sticking out around the edges inside and away from the edges to avoid sewing them together in clumps.) Repeat for the other head piece.

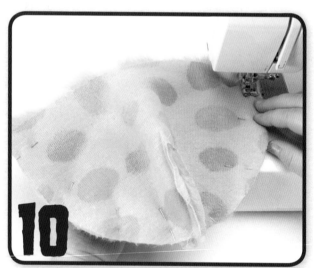

Unfold the two head pieces, and pin them right sides together. Sew around the dome and point, leaving the bottom edge unsewn.

Pin the body section inside the head section, right sides together. I find the easiest way to do this is to place the unsewn edges of the openings of the two pieces together while the feet assembly is still inside out, with the top of the head pointing away from the tips of the feet. Then I tuck the feet assembly down inside the head a bit, as shown, and pin around the edges.

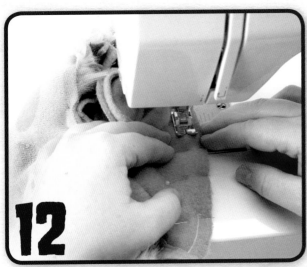

Sew the two pieces together, leaving a 2" (5cm) gap in the seam for turning it right side out.

Turn the monster right side out through the gap you left in the seam. Make sure to poke the feet all the way out.

Cut a tiny hole in the face of the monster where you want an eye to go. Place the eye in the hole and then attach the eye backing on the inside of the monster.

Stuff your *Basic Beastie* with polyester fiberfill, making sure he is nice and plump. Close the opening using a ladder stitch. To do this, thread a needle and tie a knot at one end. Stitch in one direction, passing the needle down through the fabric on one side of the opening and up through a corresponding spot on the other side. Make your stitches as evenly spaced as possible to avoid puckering. Here, I've used red thread to make my stitches easier for you to see, but for your own project, choose a color that will blend in well with your fabric.

Pull on both ends of the thread to tighten your stitches. The two fabrics should draw together.

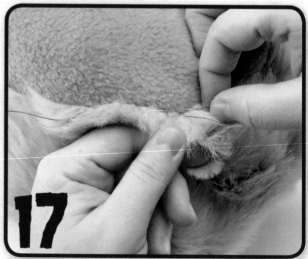

Sew back in the other direction using a ladder stitch again. Pull the fur out of the way of your stitches as you go to avoid sewing it down unnecessarily.

Pull tight, and tie a knot.

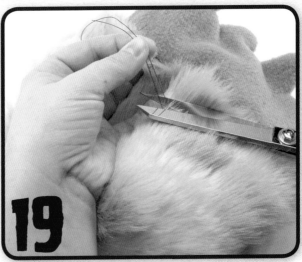

Thread the needle with the tail of the thread. Push the needle into the body of the monster and all the way through to the other side. Snip the thread close to the body so it disappears back inside (but be careful not to snip the fur in the process).

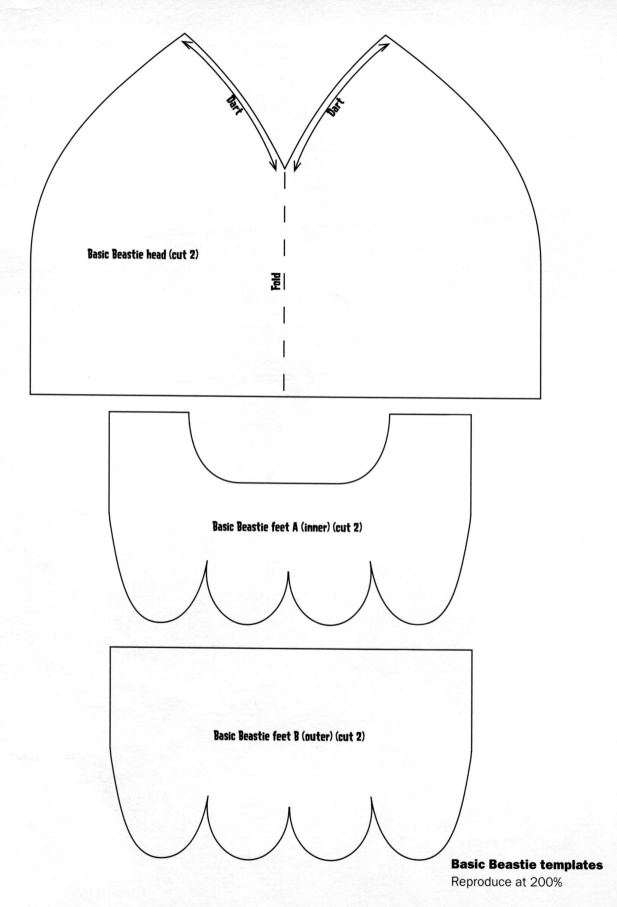

Basic Beastie head (cut 2)

Dart

Dart

Fold

Basic Beastie feet A (inner) (cut 2)

Basic Beastie feet B (outer) (cut 2)

Basic Beastie templates
Reproduce at 200%

BITING BEASTIE

This SPBB (Single Purple Biting Beastie) is in search of a good time. OK, so she's a little lacking in the eye department. Fortunately, for her, she's got a nasty assortment of head warts, which are attractive and highly aromatic to beasties of the male persuasion. Add to that her razor-sharp, bucktoothy grin and crazy mess of purple face fur, and *Biting Beastie* is never lacking for company on a Saturday night. Likes: bathtub rings, hairy backs and peach schnapps. Dislikes: negativity.

the DEVOURER

This monster pillow cover is a hollow shell of a beast. He thrives on boring, dull old pillows and gobbles up any he may see in his path. He is especially satisfied after a meal of beige and tattered twenty-year-old pillow. Sometimes he can even eat two or three old pillows at once! After eating his favorite meal, he sits quietly on a couch waiting for an unsuspecting victim to bring him along his favorite dessert—a remote control!

materials & tools

Note: These measurements will cover a pillow that is 19" (48cm) square. Add more if your pillow is larger.

Scissors

20" × 43" (51cm × 109cm) fun fur

20" × 23" (51cm × 58cm) lining fabric

20" × 4" (51cm × 10cm) red fleece

Pencil or fabric marker

Circle template

9" × 8" (23cm × 20cm) white felt

8" × 4" (20cm × 10cm) black felt

Pins

Sewing machine (optional)

Sewing needle

Matching thread

Polyester fiberfill

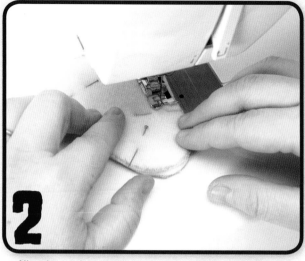

Measure the pillow you want to cover. Cut out from the fun fur a square or rectangle that is 1" (3cm) longer and wider than your pillow. This will be the back of your pillow.

For the top of the monster face on the front of your pillow, cut out a rectangle of fun fur that is 1" (3cm) wider than your pillow and half the height of the first piece you cut. For a 19" (48cm) pillow like I've used here, it will be 20" × 10" (51cm × 25cm).

For the bottom of the monster face, cut out a rectangle of fun fur that is 7" (18cm) shorter than the back piece and the same width. If using a 19" (48cm) pillow, it will be 20" × 13" (51cm × 33cm).

From your lining fabric, cut two pieces exactly the same sizes as the top and bottom of the front. Any sort of fabric can be used for the lining—an old shirt, a T-shirt, another piece of clothing or a favorite cotton print. If you choose a fabric that's thin, like those listed above, you'll have an easier time sewing through the layers. Once, I used an old men's shirt as the source of the fabric for my lining. One of the pieces happened to have a pocket on it, so I ended up with a secret pocket on the inside of my pillow for hiding monstery messages.

Cut from the red fleece a rectangle for the lip that is the same width as your other pieces and 4" (10cm) tall.

Cut out six teeth (see template on page 29) from white felt.

Using the circle template, cut two 1½" (4cm) circles from white felt and two 3½" (9cm) circles from black felt.

Align the teeth pieces in pairs, wrong sides together, and pin. Use a ⅜" (10mm) seam allowance, and back tack at both ends of every seam from here on out unless otherwise noted. Sew around the curved edge of each tooth. Do not sew the straight edge.

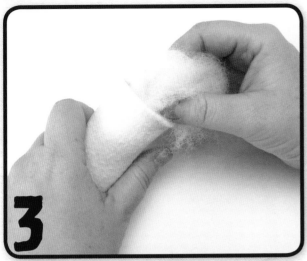

Cut small notches in the seam allowance around each tooth curve, taking care not to cut your seam. Turn each tooth right side out, and stuff lightly with polyester fiberfill. Don't overfill the teeth, because that will make it harder to sew them in place.

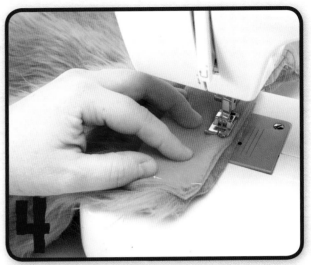

Fold the lip piece in half lengthwise with the right side facing out to make a long, skinny lip. Pin the folded lip to the top edge of the bottom front of the pillow cover, aligning the raw edges. Tuck the fur hairs inward as you pin. Stitch across to join these two pieces, using seam allowance of about ½" (6mm).

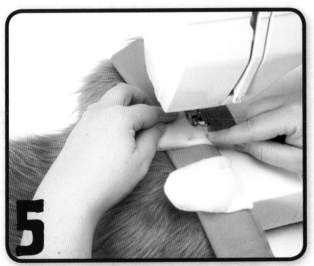

Arrange the teeth on top of the lip, and align the raw edges. Space them unevenly for a more monstery, gap-toothed look, or evenly if your monster happens to have a good orthodontist. Pin in place. Sew the teeth on using a ¼" (6mm) seam allowance.

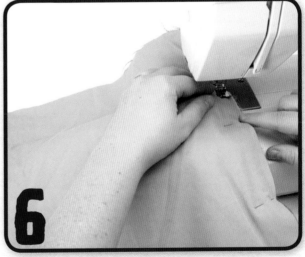

Place the lining for the bottom front on top of the lips and teeth, aligning the entire piece with the fur piece beneath. The right side of the lining should be facing the furry side of the fur. If you have any secret pockets on this piece, they should be facing the fur. Pin across the top. From bottom to top, the layers of fabric should be as follows: fur, lip, teeth, lining. Stitch across the top edge using a ⅜" (10mm) seam allowance, enclosing the lips and teeth between the fur and lining. Pin the other piece of lining to the top front fur piece, wrong sides together, and sew it along the bottom edge (that is, along one of the long edges).

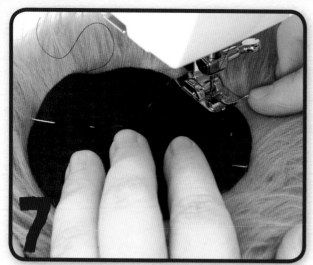

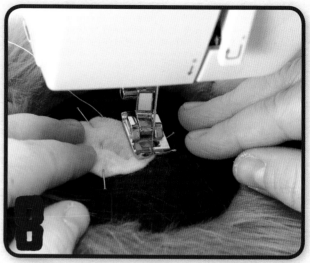

Turn the top piece of the pillow face right side out. Pin the black circles 2" (5cm) in and 2" (5cm) down from the upper edges of the front face of the monster. Sew them in place with a zigzag stitch, being careful to keep the fur out of the way as you sew.

Pin and sew the white pupil onto the black eye with a zigzag stitch (I like to place my pupils a bit off center to give the finished face a little more character).

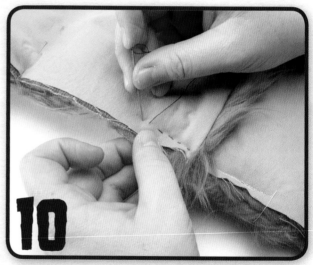

Pin all the layers together in this order: back fur (right side up), bottom half of the front (lining facing up), top of the front (lining facing up). Here I've pulled back the top half of the front so you can see where the teeth are positioned underneath.

Sew all the layers together around the four edges of the pillow. If your machine won't sew through certain spots where the fabric layers are particularly thick, handsew those areas. Make sure you use strong thread. All that's left now is to turn your monster right side out and feed him his first delectable pillow!

Monster Tip

Strong thread is especially important for items intended for kids or that will get a lot of use (like a couch pillow). For extra durability when sewing monsters, choose a heavy-duty coated thread.

Tooth (cut 6)

Devourer tooth templates
Reproduce at 100%

GNAWMITTS

Watch out, because you never know what your hands might do once inside these scary monster mitts. Just when you think your hands are getting cozy and warm, the mitts will commandeer your hands to do things they might not otherwise. Don't be surprised if they start nibbling on strangers' babies' noses. Do expect them to sniff out a fine basket of fruits and chocolates and take one bite out of each piece, leaving teeth marks all over everything. It would also not be considered unusual for your hands to attack each other constantly.

materials & tools

Pencil or fabric marker

Scissors

18" × 11" (46cm × 28cm) green fleece

11" × 11" (28cm × 28cm) fuchsia fleece

Iron

HeatnBond

Small amount of yellow fleece

Circle template

Small amount of black fleece

Pins

White rickrack

Sewing machine (optional)

Sewing needle

Matching thread

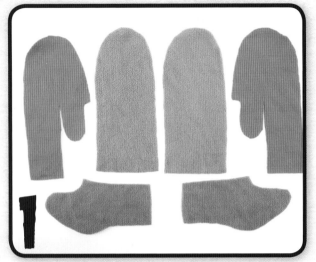

Cut out all the pattern pieces (see templates on page 35); you'll need two of each. If you are using a fabric with a right and wrong side, flip the template when cutting the mitten palm and mitten thumb—you'll want a right and left Gnawmitt.

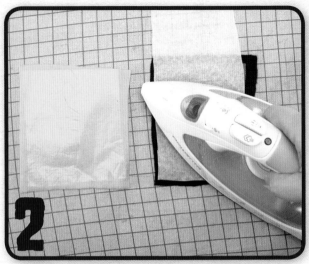

Iron the HeatnBond onto the back of both yellow-fleece eye fabrics. Follow the manufacturer's instructions.

Using the circle template, trace circles of varying sizes onto the back of the yellow fleece (I used circles of sizes ranging between ¾" [2cm] and 1⅜" [3cm]). Trace black circles to fit inside the yellow ones as pupils. Make as many or as few eyes as you like. The mitten-back template shows one possible assortment. Remember to make enough for two mittens.

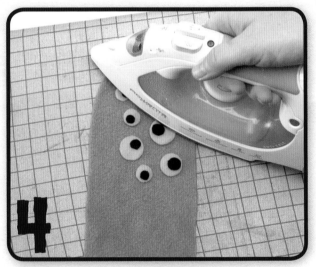

Cut out the circles, and iron the larger yellow ones onto the finger area of both mitten backs. Then iron the black ones inside them (see the template on page 35 as a placement guide, if you like). Remember to make one mitten back the mirror image of the other if you want them to match as left and right hands. Continue to follow the manufacturer's instructions for using the HeatnBond.

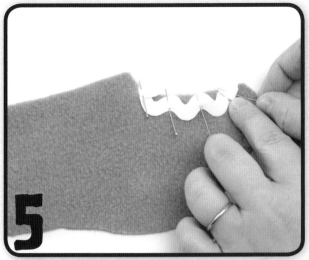

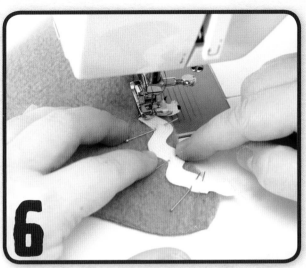

From here you'll work on one mitten at a time. Pin the strip of rickrack for the teeth along the right side edge of one mitten thumb where indicated on the template, with one end near the tip of the thumb. The points of the rickrack facing toward the inside of the fabric will become the points of the teeth when the mitten is sewn together and turned right side out.

Sew along the center of the rickrack strip, leaving the rickrack points free.

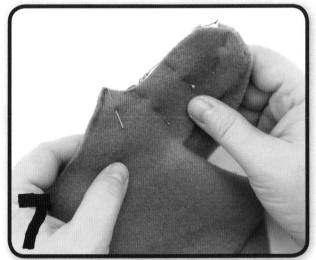

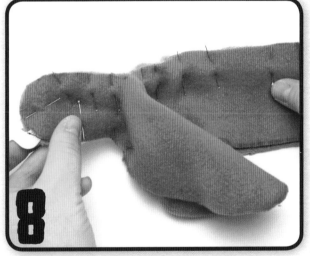

Pin the edge of the mitten thumb with the rickrack to the edge of the thumb section of the mitten palm, matching up the tips of the thumbs (here, I've folded the wrist end of the mitten palm back and out of the way). The two thumb sections don't match exactly and are not meant to. You must finesse the edges into place. To do so, place one pin at the tip of the thumb, after lining up the edges as best you can. Next, maneuver the little corner points (marked *A* on the templates on page 35) of both pieces together, and place a pin there. Finally, space a couple more pins along the edge. Make sure the ends of the rickrack stick out from between the two pieces.

Pin down the other edge of the thumb, finessing it as you did the first edge in Step 7. When you get to the base of the deep *V* in the mitten palm piece, fold the unpinned flap of the palm down along the edge of the thumb along which you're working as shown in the photo. Pin the corners of the two fabrics (marked *B* on the templates) together down near the wrist. Finesse that edge into place as you pin along the intervening space.

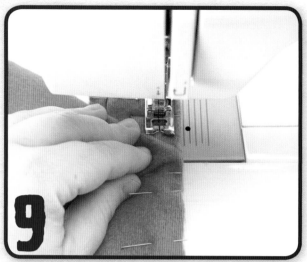

Sew the two pieces together around the edges from point *A* to point *B* (see the templates on page 35). When you get to the bump near the thumb, hold it down carefully as you sew.

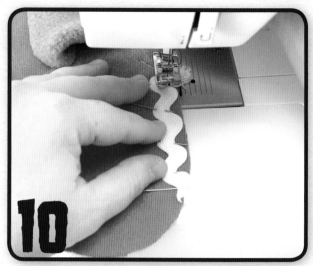

Pin and sew the second set of teeth to the fuchsia fleece (see the templates on page 35). You now have the entire bottom half of the mitten together—the palm and the thumb combined.

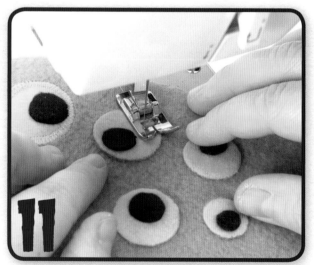

Set aside the bottom of the mitten. Using a zigzag stitch, sew around the edges of the circles of both sizes, securing them to the mitten back.

Now it's time to pin the mitten back to the rest of the assembly (I arranged the pieces so the eyes on the back are nearest the edge of the palm with the rickrack). Place the mitten back right sides together, catching the second rickrack piece between the edges of the fabrics. Start by pinning into place the two corners down by the wrist, and then pin the very tips of the fingers together. Place pins all the way around the edge of the mitten, finessing it in place. Sew together. Repeat Steps 5–12 for the second mitten. When pinning and sewing the mitten palm and mitten thumb pieces together, make sure you arrange them so you are making a mirror image of the first set. Turn right side out and allow to gnaw!

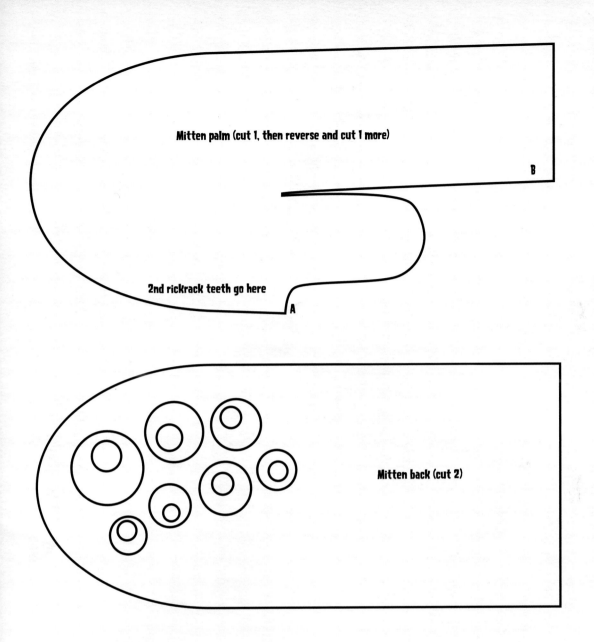

Mitten palm (cut 1, then reverse and cut 1 more)

B

2nd rickrack teeth go here

A

Mitten back (cut 2)

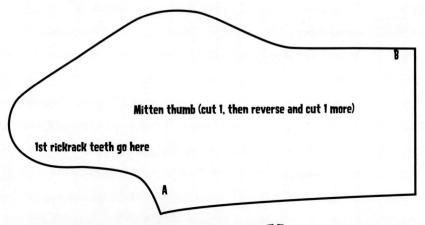

Mitten thumb (cut 1, then reverse and cut 1 more)

B

1st rickrack teeth go here

A

Gnawmitts templates
Reproduce at 182%

the COLOSSAL GIGANTOHUGGAH

This monster is almost human-sized. As a matter of fact, if you happen to be a small human, he might even be bigger than you. Due to this fact, this monster makes a very good stand-in when you have to leave the room for a minute. Let's just say you want to get more of those pigs in a blanket before they are all gone, but you also don't want to lose your seat. Just ask *Gigantohuggah* to sit in your chair until you come back. Nobody is gonna mess with him. He is always happy to fill in for humans temporarily and is actually a very nice monster. It might be wise to take him to every party you go to. If you don't, there's no guarantee he will stay nice.

materials & tools

Pencil or fabric marker

Scissors

19½" × 15" (50cm × 38cm) striped fleece

Small amount of fuchsia, green, dark green, yellow and turquoise fleece

2 pieces of 7¼" × 1½" (18cm × 4cm) white fleece

Circle template

6" (15cm) square each of pink, blue, green and yellow fun fur

3 yds. (3m) brown fun fur

Pins

Sewing machine (optional)

Sewing needle

Matching thread

Polyester fiberfill or foam peanuts

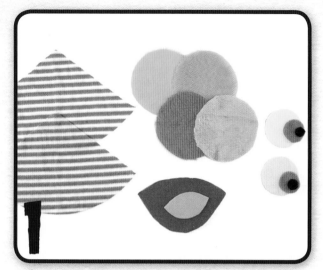

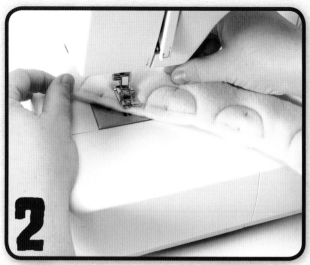

Cut out your pattern pieces (except for the teeth). You'll need:

· Two horns from striped fleece (see the template on page 41)

· A pair of eye pieces in each of the following diameters and each pair in a different fleece color: 3¼" (8cm), 2" (5cm), 1" (3cm)

· Two mouth pieces (design your own—my large mouth measures 7¾" × 4½" (20cm × 11cm), the smaller tongue piece 4" × 2" (10cm × 5cm)

· Four 6" (15cm) circles for the palms, each in a different color of fleece

· Four brown fur body pieces measuring 12" (30cm) across the top, 16" (41cm) across the bottom and 21" (53cm) down both sides (see the construction diagram on page 41)

· One brown fur top 12" × 12" (30cm × 30cm)

· One brown fur bottom 16" × 16" (41cm × 41cm)

· Two arms 16½" × 14" (40cm × 36cm)

· Two legs 16½" × 18½" (40cm × 47cm)

Pin the two pieces of felt for the teeth together. Trace four teeth (or however many you want to fit in your monster's mouth) onto the top piece (see the template on page 41). Sew along the curved, traced lines, leaving the straight lines unsewn.

Cut out the teeth, leaving ¼" (6mm) of fabric outside the stitching. On the side that wasn't sewn, cut right on the traced line. Be careful not to cut into your stitching.

Turn the teeth right side out. Trim off the parts of the seam allowance that stick out above the top edge on each tooth.

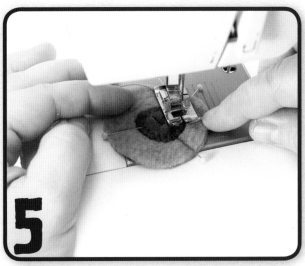

Pin the smallest eye piece to the medium one, and sew it in place with a zigzag stitch.

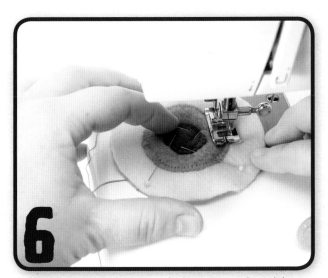

Pin the medium eye piece to the large one, and sew it in place with a zigzag stitch.

Arrange the brown body pieces but don't sew them together yet. Mark 4" (10cm) circles on the wrong sides of the fabric for the arms, legs and horns per the diagram on page 41. Cut out the circles. Arrange the pieces of the face on the right side of the front of the body as desired. Sew in place with a zigzag stitch. Sew the large mouth piece before the tongue. Stitch across the top of the teeth to keep them in place.

Fold each limb in half lengthwise, right sides together. Sew a seam along the long edges of each to make tubes.

Pin a hand circle into the hole at one end of each limb, right side facing in. The right side of the edges of the palm circle will be in contact with the right side of the arm fabric edge around the hole, as shown.

Sew the hand in place with the palm facing down on the bed of the sewing machine.

Fold the horn in half, right sides together, to form a cone. Pin it and stitch down the straight side.

Sew the body pieces together one piece at a time, right sides together, forming a cross shape, like the construction diagram. Once this is complete, turn the arms and legs right side out. Pin one arm into an armhole so the seam faces the back of the monster. Sew in place. Repeat for all the limbs and the two horns. Sew everything shut right sides together, except for the top of the head, to form an inside-out box with the limbs on the inside. Turn the monster right side out through the opening at the top of the monster. Stuff the monster with the polyester fiberfill or the foam peanuts. Handsew the top of the head shut.

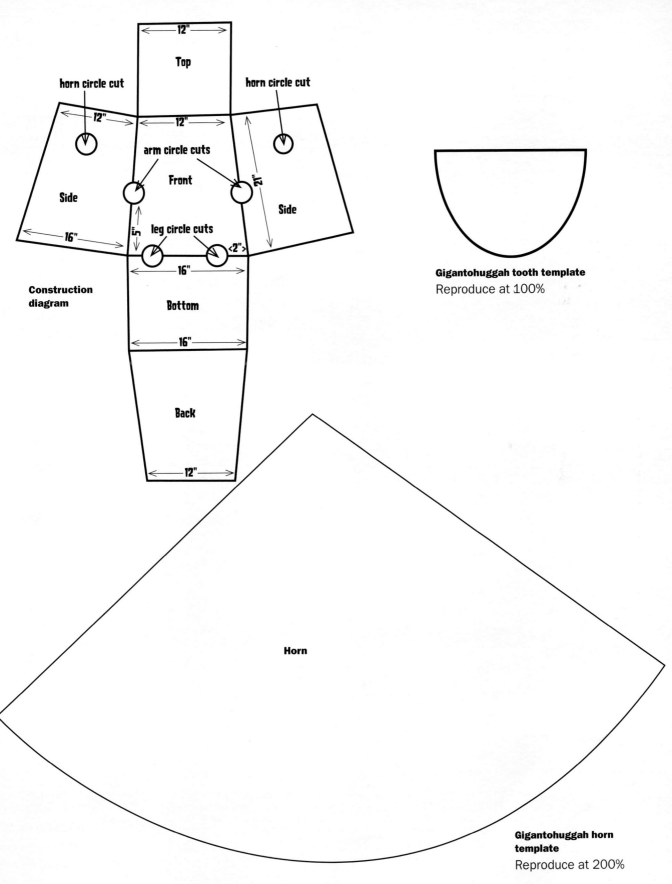

Construction diagram

12" — Top

horn circle cut — horn circle cut

12" — 12"

arm circle cuts

Front

Side — 21" — Side

16" — 5" — leg circle cuts — <2">

16"

Bottom

16"

Back

12"

Gigantohuggah tooth template
Reproduce at 100%

Horn

Gigantohuggah horn template
Reproduce at 200%

beastish BANNERS

materials & tools

Decorate your next party with creepy monster flags. With their big googly eyes, they will stare at everyone long and hard—possibly so hard they will make some people uncomfortable. Those people may leave, but the cool people will stay. And then you'll know that only the "best, most coolest" people will be at your party. Then you can really have lots of fun!

Pencil or fabric marker

Scissors

16" × 9" (41cm × 23cm) fabric for each flag panel (you'll need extra if you're using stripes on the diagonal)

White felt

Black felt

Pins

Sewing machine (optional)

Sewing needle

Matching thread

Pointy object

Iron

HeatnBond

Hot-glue gun

15¾" (40mm) googly eyes

Bias tape or enough fabric to make 2" (5cm) strip long enough for the length of flags you desire.

Bias-tape-making tool (optional)

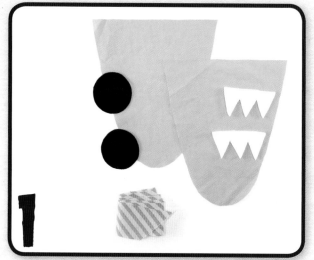

Cut out all the flag pieces (see the template on page 47). Each flag will need a front and a back. Cut out as many pairs as you like. Five pairs makes a banner about 44" (112cm) long. Cut out two teeth pieces from white felt for each flag. Decide how many eyes you'd like to have on each flag (I alternated one-eyed and two-eyed flags), and cut a 2½" (6cm) black felt circle for each eye.

Align two teeth pieces on top of one of the flag panels (see the template on page 47 for placement). Place the other flag panel on top of them, with the two flag panels aligned. Pin the four pieces together.

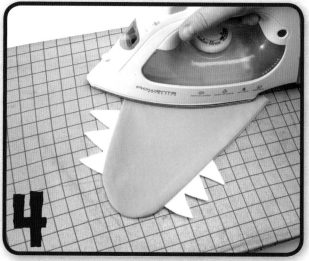

Stitch around the curved edge of the flag using a ⅜" (10mm) seam allowance and back tacking at the beginning and end of the seam. Leave the straight edge unsewn. Cut small notches in the seam allowance on the flag between the two teeth pieces, taking care not to cut your seam.

Turn the flag right side out. Use a pointy (but not sharp) object to poke the seam from the inside and turn out the tip of the flag as much as possible. Iron it flat.

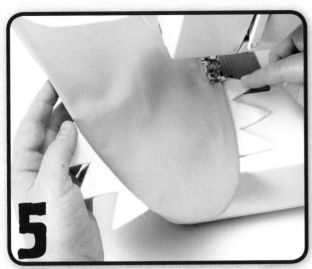

Topstitch ⅛" (3mm) from the edge around the curved edge of the flag, continuing to leave the top open. Iron flat. Snip the little corners of the inside seam allowance that stick out the top of the flag in order to make the top straight.

Follow the manufacturer's instructions on the HeatnBond to adhere the black circles in place for the eyes. Use a hot-glue gun to glue the googly eyes on top. Repeat Steps 1–6 for as many flags as you want.
Note: If using premade bias binding to attach the flags, skip Steps 7–9.

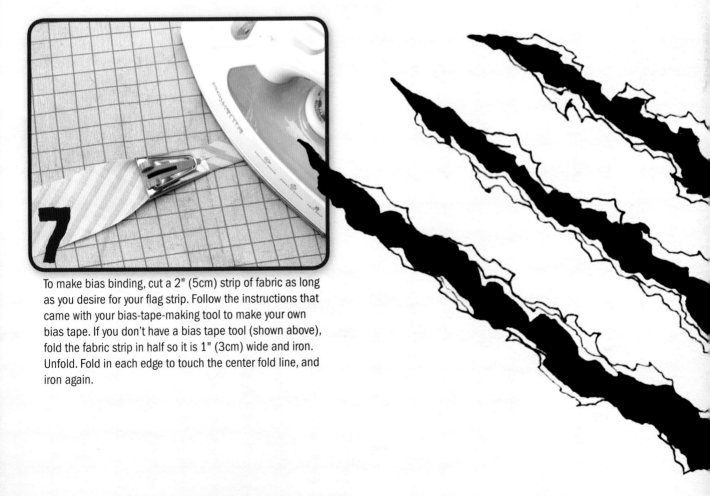

To make bias binding, cut a 2" (5cm) strip of fabric as long as you desire for your flag strip. Follow the instructions that came with your bias-tape-making tool to make your own bias tape. If you don't have a bias tape tool (shown above), fold the fabric strip in half so it is 1" (3cm) wide and iron. Unfold. Fold in each edge to touch the center fold line, and iron again.

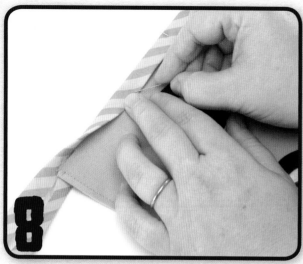

Find the center of the fabric strip by folding the whole thing in half lengthwise, and mark it with a pin. Place the top edge of one flag along the line where the two binding halves meet, matching its center to the center of the bias tape or fabric where you marked it. Fold the bias tape over the edge of the flag's top edge, then pin in place.

Straight stitch the binding to the flag. Repeat Steps 8–9 for as many flags as you have made. I left a little over 1" (13cm) between each flag.

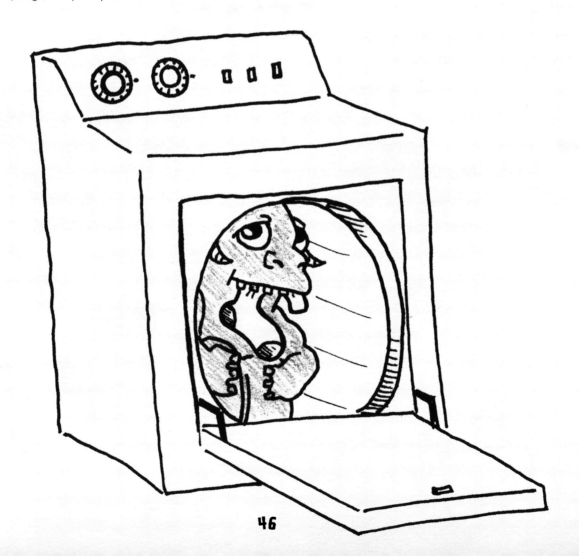

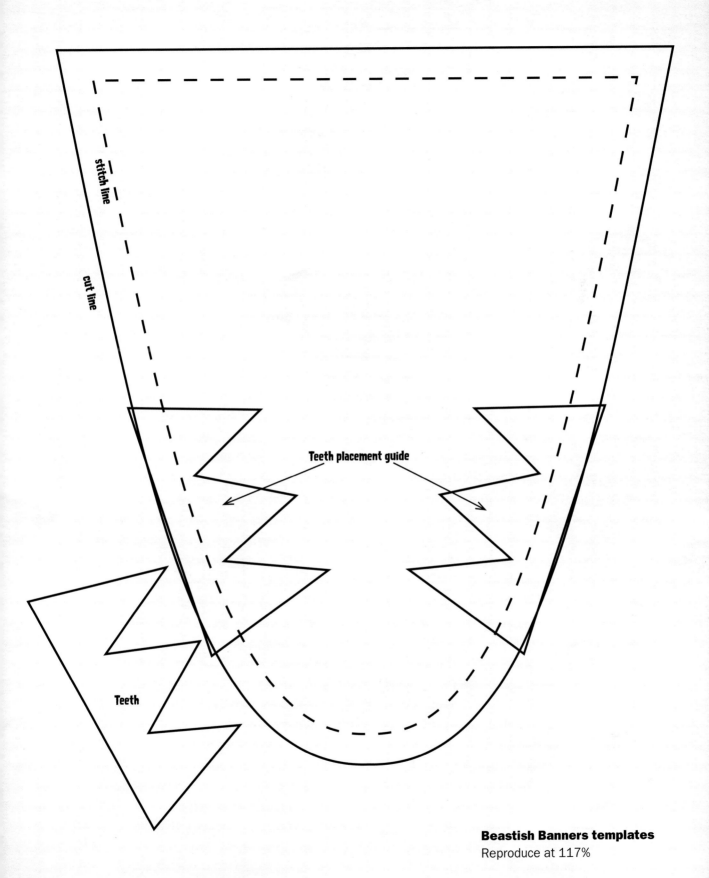

stitch line

cut line

Teeth placement guide

Teeth

Beastish Banners templates
Reproduce at 117%

CHAPTER 2
THE HAIR OF THE BEAST

Some of my best fiendish friends are knitted—monsters really like being stuck with needles, the masochistic little beasties. In the pages to come, you'll meet some of my favorite fiber monsters, in the form of knit, crochet, felt embroidery and plastic canvas needlepoint, with the occasional pom-pom and Swarovski crystal thrown in. (Hey, even monsters appreciate a little bling now and then!) It's a delectable sampler of projects for those of you who stand, mouth watering, in the yarn aisle of your local craft store, resisting (or not) the urge to roll in all the pretty colors and nubby yarns. Mmmm…nice.

These smaller-scale meanies are perfect for adding a touch of whimsy, warmth and weirdness to your home, hut or even office—if you are employed at a monster-friendly workplace.

nom nom NOMSTERS

by Anna Hrachovec

These monsters greet each other by eating each other! The Big guy mostly likes to greet the Medium guy, and the Medium guy mostly likes to greet the little Baby guy. Sometimes the Big guy likes to greet three Baby guys at once! Hello! Hello! Hello! Trouble occurs when Medium tries to greet Big. That's a mouthful and generally considered to be quite rude in Nomster culture. Poor Baby Nomster hasn't learned how to get his chomp on yet. He is happy to be greeted by Medium or Big, for now. After a long morning of saying hello to each other, the Nomsters will prepare for a nap. Big, Medium and Baby like to cozy up and go for a snooze in a hollow stump. When they wake, they will start greeting and eating each other all over again.

materials & tools

YARN
Small amounts of Koigu Premium Merino (100% wool, 1¾ oz [50g] and 170 yds [155m]) in each of colors no. 2130 Blue (A), no. 2132 Green (B), no. 2231 Light Pink (C), no. 1200 Yellow (D) and no. 2400 Black (E)

NEEDLES
One set of four size US 1 (2.25mm) double-pointed needles

NOTIONS
Tapestry needle

Small amount of polyester fiberfill

GAUGE
36 sts and 56 rows = 4" (10cm) in St st

FINISHED MEASUREMENTS
Big Nomster: 2" (5cm) tall,

Medium Nomster: 1½" (4cm) tall

Baby Nomster: 1¼" (3cm) tall

Standard Knitting Abbreviations

[ ] repeat instructions within brackets as many times as directed

BO bind off

CO cast on

dpn(s) double-pointed needle(s)

k knit

kfb knit through the front and back loop

k2tog knit two together

rem remain(ing)

rnd(s) round(s)

st(s) stitch(es)

St st Stockinette stitch

Baby Nomster Body

CO 6 sts onto 3 needles and join to work in a rnd.
Rnd 1: [Kfb] 6 times—12 sts. Place marker.
Rnd 2: [Kfb, k1] 6 times—18 sts.
Rnd 3: Knit.
Rnd 4: [Kfb, k2] 6 times—24 sts.
Rnds 5–14: Knit 10 rnds.
Rnd 15: [K2tog, k2] 6 times—18 sts.
Rnd 16: Knit.
Rnd 17: [K2tog, k1] 6 times—12 sts.
Stuff before continuing.
Rnd 18: [K2tog] 6 times—6 sts.
Break yarn and draw tightly through sts using a tapestry needle.

Medium Nomster Body

CO 6 sts onto 3 needles and join to work in a rnd.
Rnd 1: [Kfb] 6 times—12 sts. Place marker.
Rnd 2: [Kfb, k1] 6 times—18 sts.
Rnd 3: Knit.
Rnd 4: [Kfb, k2] 6 times—24 sts.
Rnd 5: Knit.
Rnd 6: [kfb, k3] 6 times—30 sts.
Rnds 7–12: Knit 6 rnds.
Rnd 13: K10, BO 10 sts, k9. At the end of this rnd, there should be 20 sts total on your needles—2 groups of 10 sts.
Rnd 14: K10, CO 10 sts using backward loop cast-on, k10—30 sts.

Monster Tip

For a backward loop cast-on, loop the yarn once around your thumb counter-clockwise, slip onto the needle, then release your thumb and gently pull the loop closed around the needle.

Monster Tip

If you substitute yarn, be sure to select a yarn of the same weight as the yarn recommended for the project. Even after checking that the recommended gauge on the yarn you plan to substitute is the same as for the yarn listed in the pattern, make sure to knit a swatch to ensure the yarn and needles you are using will produce the correct gauge.

Rnds 15–18: Knit 4 rnds.
Rnd 19: [K2tog, k3] 6 times—24 sts.
Rnd 20: Knit.
Rnd 21: [K2tog, k2] 6 times—18 sts.
Rnd 22: Knit.
Rnd 23: [K2tog, k1] 6 times—12 sts.
Rnd 24: [K2tog] 6 times—6 sts.
Break yarn and draw tightly through sts using a tapestry needle.

Big Nomster Body
CO 6 sts onto 3 needles and join to work in a rnd.
Rnd 1: [Kfb] 6 times—12 sts. Place marker.
Rnd 2: [Kfb, k1] 6 times—18 sts.
Rnd 3: Knit.
Rnd 4: [Kfb, k2] 6 times—24 sts.
Rnd 5: Knit.
Rnd 6: [Kfb, k3] 6 times—30 sts.
Rnd 7: Knit.
Rnd 8: [Kfb, k4] 6 times—36 sts.
Rnds 9–15: Knit 7 rnds.
Rnd 16: K12, BO 12, k11. At the end of this rnd, there should be 24 sts total on your needles—2 groups of 12 sts.
Rnd 17: K12, CO 12 sts using backward loop cast-on, k12—36 sts.
Rnds 18–22: Knit 5 rnds.
Rnd 23: [K2tog, k4] 6 times—30 sts.
Rnd 24: Knit.
Rnd 25: [K2tog, k3] 6 times—24 sts.
Rnd 26: [K2tog, k2] 6 times—18 sts.
Rnd 27: Knit
Rnd 28: [K2tog, k1] 6 times—12 sts.
Rnd 29: [K2tog] 6 times—6 sts.
Break yarn and draw tightly through sts using a tapestry needle.

Arms and Legs (same for Medium and Big Nomsters)
Turn body upside down and pick up and knit 3 sts from body. Arms should be placed just under and toward the edges of the mouth, and legs should be placed at the bottom of the body and under the arms.

Slide sts down to the right side of the needle, and pull the working yarn around the back from the left side to knit the first rnd as an I-cord.

Rnd 1: [Kfb] 3 times—6 sts.
Distribute the sts onto 3 needles to work in a rnd.
Knit 2 rnds.
If there is enough room, insert a small amount of stuffing into the appendage.
Break yarn and draw tightly through sts.

Ears (same for all sizes)
With the body right side up, pick up and knit 3 sts from the top of the head, set just to the outside of the closed-off sts at top.
Knit 2 rows of I-cord.
Break yarn and draw tightly through sts.

Teeth (same for all sizes)
Pick up and knit 3 sts with Yellow. For Medium and Big Nomsters, pick up sts right on the edge of the mouth. For Baby Nomster, turn the body upside down, and pick up sts in the middle of the body.
Knit 2 rows of I-cord.
Break yarn and draw tightly through sts.

Eyes (same for all sizes)

With Black yarn and tapestry needle, wrap 1 knitted st with 4–6 horizontal sts of Black yarn.

Mouth (Baby Nomster only)

For Baby Nomster's mouth, use Black yarn and tapestry needle to embroider one long st just above the tooth.

Weave in loose ends.

Here are the three completed Nomsters. Use this picture as a guide for placing the limbs and embroidering the faces.

VARIATION
WOM

by Daniel Yuhas

Woms are soft-spoken, reclusive creatures that provide more than enough of their own company. It is actually quite rare to see a clan out in the open. Legend has it that Woms originated from a serious breach of Nomster etiquette, when a Nom Nom met a Magic 8 Ball. It was love at first sight (gulp!)…at least for the Nom Nom. The unrequited love affair left behind a small clan of Woms in magical rainbow colors. Keep the Woms on your good side, and they will guard your car keys, precious jewels and love notes to yourself. But don't let their big eyes and vaguely froglike expression lull you into a false sense of security—cross them and they will hold your precious belongings hostage. All you can do at that point is "Ask Again Later."

cake monster CUTE-ILITY pack

by Twinkie Chan

materials & tools

This little cake likes to hang out at your side. Don't worry, she won't get sticky, gooey frosting all over you, but she does have a scary monster power. She can hypnotize you with her cute beams, which means if she actually were slathering you with frosting, you totally wouldn't care. She also has the power to eat only your most important items. Here are a few things she finds most delicious: your driver's license, lip balm and hundred-dollar bills. Again, don't worry, you can just take them out of her belly whenever you need them. But FYI: She'll most likely use her cute beams to try to trick you out of your hundreds. One other thing that you should know about this tasty little treat: She has a motto and isn't afraid to shout it—"Bring back the fanny pack!"

- 1 skein Cascade 220 (100% wool, 220 yds. [201m]) in Cotton Candy (Frosting Color, or FC)
- 1 skein Cascade 220 (100% wool, 220 yds. [201m]) in Natural (Main Color, or MC)
- 1 skein Cascade 220 (100% wool, 220 yds. [201m]) in Sunflower (Cake Color, or CC)
- 1 skein (or small amount) Cascade 220 (100% wool, 220 yards [201m]) in Christmas Red (Berry Color, or BC)
- 1 size K (6.5mm) crochet hook
- 1 tapestry needle
- White zippered or regular pillowcase (optional)
- Rubber band
- Washing machine
- Laundry detergent
- Matching thread for MC
- Sewing needle
- 1 9" (23cm) zipper that matches MC
- Pins
- 2 large black buttons
- Matching thread for buttons
- Small amount of green ribbon no more than 9mm wide (enough for three small bows)
- Matching thread for green ribbon
- Mini pom-poms (optional)
- Fabri-Tac
- Seed beads or bugle beads
- 15 3mm Swarovski flat-back crystals in Light Topaz
- Gem-Tac

Crochet Pattern

You'll start by crocheting the piece in its entirety, and then you'll pop it in the washing machine to felt it. Felting is the process of turning a woolen crocheted or knitted project into a sturdier, nonstretchy, non-hole-y piece of felt by shrinking the project with hot water, agitation and soap. You can do this by hand or in a washing machine. I find there are pros and cons to both methods, but for the sake of ease, this pattern will use the machine method. Your yarn needs to be 100% wool that is not superwash.

When you felt crocheted pouches and purses, you don't have to worry about the gaps between your stitches or excessive stretching. Also, you get a unique, fuzzy texture out of the process! When preparing a project for felting, crochet more loosely than usual with a larger hook. A more loosely crocheted piece will felt more nicely because there is room for the fibers to rub together. Your final product will be smaller than your initial crocheted piece.

The fun part of this particular pattern is that you can pretty much choose any colors you like to remind you of your favorite cake!

Standard Crochet

Abbreviations

ch(s) chain(s)

dc double crochet

dec decrease

dtr double triple crochet

hdc half double crochet

hk hook

lp(s) loop(s)

rnd(s) round(s)

sc single crochet

sk skip

sl slip

st(s) stitch(es)

tr triple crochet

Pattern Stitches

Shell: Sk 1 st, work 5 dc into next st, sk 1 st, sl st into next st.

Drip: Ch 6 away from your main piece. Turn and sk first 2 chs, and then work 4 hdc evenly down remaining chs. Sk 1 st on your main piece, and then sl st in the next st to join back.

Main Pouch, Panel A

With MC, ch 29 loosely.

Row 1: Sk 2 chs, then work hdc evenly across —27 sts.

Rows 2–15: Ch 2, turn (counts as first hdc here and throughout). Work hdc evenly across—27 sts. Cut yarn and weave in all ends using your tapestry needle.

Main Pouch, Panel B

Repeat Main Pouch Panel A, except before beginning your ch 29, leave two arms' lengths of yarn free to sew Panel A and Panel B together. These two pieces will form the foundation of your zipper pouch. Weave in your tail from the end of the piece.

Arms and Legs (make 4)

This pattern is worked in continuous rnds.
Using CC, leave about 12" (30cm) of yarn free and ch 3.

Monster Tip

If you substitute yarn, be sure to select a yarn of the same weight as the yarn recommended for the project. Even after checking that the recommended gauge on the yarn you plan to substitute is the same as for the yarn listed in the pattern, make sure to knit a swatch to ensure the yarn and needles you are using will produce the correct gauge.

Rnd 1: Work 12 hdc into first ch.

Rnds 2–8: Work 1 hdc into the first hdc you made, and continue to work hdc evenly around, creating a small tube.

Rnd 9: Sc in next hdc, sl st in next st and cut yarn, leaving about a 12" (30cm) tail for sewing later. Thread your tapestry needle with your beginning yarn tail, and if there is a hole created by your initial 12 hdcs, sew this hole closed and weave in the end.

Belt Loops (make 2)

With MC, leave 12" (30cm) of yarn and ch 18.

Row 1: Sk 2 chs, and then work hdc evenly across—16 sts.

Rows 2–4: Ch 2, turn. Work hdc evenly across—16 sts.

Cut yarn, leaving a 12" (30cm) tail for sewing.

Frosting Face/Pocket, Panel C

With FC, leave an arm's length of yarn and ch 29 loosely. You will use the beginning length of yarn for sewing pieces together later.

Row 1: Sk 2 chs, then work hdc evenly across—27 sts.

Rows 2–7: Ch 2, turn. Work hdc evenly across—27 sts.

Row 8: Ch 1, turn. Work 1 shell, 1 drip, 3 shells, 1 drip, sl st, 1 drip and 1 shell. Break off. Weave in end.

Frosting Face/Bottom, Panel D

With FC, leave about two arms' lengths of yarn and ch 29 loosely. You will use the beginning length of yarn for sewing pieces together later.

Row 1: Sk 2 chs, then work hdc evenly across—27 sts.

Row 2: Ch 1, turn. Work 1 drip, 2 shells, 1 drip, 1 shell, 1 drip, sl st, 1 drip, 1 shell and 1 drip, then break off. Weave in end.

Strawberries (make 3)

With BC, ch 4.

Row 1: Sk 1 ch, sc in each remaining ch—3 sc.

Row 2: Ch 1, turn. Work 2 sc in first sc, 1 sc, 2 sc in last sc—5 sc.

Rows 3–4: Ch 1, turn. Sc in each sc across—5 sc.

Row 5: Ch 1, turn. Work 2 sc in first sc, 1 sc in each of next 3 sc, 2 sc in last sc—7 sc.

Rows 6–7: Ch 1, turn. Sc in each sc across—7 sc.

Row 8: Ch 1, turn. Dec over next 2 sc, 1 sc each of next 3 sc, dec over next 2 sc—5 sc.

Row 9: Ch 1, turn. Dec over next 2 sc, 1 sc, dec over next 2 sc. Don't turn—3 sc.

Sl st evenly around until you meet back up with the beginning of Row 9. Sl st in the first sc of Row 9 and then cut your yarn, leaving about 16" (41cm) of tail for sewing later. Weave in your end from the beginning chain.

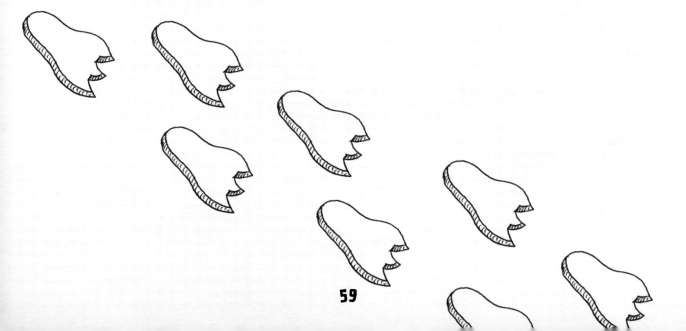

Assembly

Place Panel A wrong side down with your last row of hdc on the top and your beginning chain on the bottom. Arrange the arms and legs on top of Panel A. You want to overlap your limbs and Panel A just enough to hide the end of your limb inside the pouch (about two rows in). Use the tails of yarn from the arms and legs to sew them in place. I'm using green yarn so you can see where I've sewn, but your stitches will be invisible. Remember not to sew all the way through Panel A, or you'll get brown spots on the back of your pouch. The sewing here doesn't have to be impeccable. You just need to hold the limbs in place. Pick up one loop of Panel A, followed by both layers of your arm or leg, with the tapestry needle.

Flip your piece over, and sew the belt loops on. Again, I'm using green yarn to show you where to sew, but your stitching will be invisible because you will be using the long tails of yarn to your sew belt loops to Panel A. As you can see, I sew two rows of stitches for extra security.

Monster Tip

When sewing together pieces for a felted project, I don't tie knots. I weave my ends back and forth invisibly through my work with the tapestry needle and cut them off. That way, a knot won't felt into a little bump! Also, don't sew too tightly, or you'll notice you'll pull holes in your crochet work. Finally, there's no need to be perfect. After everything shrinks down, you won't be able to see your stitches or sewing. You are just providing a good anchor for the felting.

Pick up Frosting Face Panel C and sew three strawberries with backstitching to the top. Make sure the right side of the last row you worked on Panel C is facing you. That way, the top of your monster's mouth will align correctly with the bottom. You will be using the extra tail of yarn from the strawberries for sewing, which will make your stitches invisible. I would attach the strawberries on either side first and do the middle one last. It can be hard to center the middle one!

Place Panel C with the strawberries on the top of Panel B (the top of Panel B is the last row you worked), and backstitch all around, using the long tail of yarn from Panel C; leave the top open (this will be your pocket). Place Panel D over the lower part of Panel B, as shown, and backstitch all the way around with the long tail from Panel D, leaving no opening. As with Panel C, make sure the right side of the last row you worked on Panel D is facing you. If you ever run out of yarn for sewing on the pieces, just weave in your end, cut off and use a new piece of yarn in the same color. No need for knots. Just weave in all your ends back and forth.

Place Panel B (with all the smaller attached pieces facing up), on top of Panel A (with the belt loops facing away and down). Panels A and B now form your main pouch, with the arms and legs sandwiched in the middle. Using the loose yarn tail from Panel B, whipstitch together the sides and bottoms of Panels A and B, leaving the top open (this is where your zipper will go later). When you get to an arm or leg, use regular backstitching to go through all the layers, and then continue whipstitching Panels A and B together. While whipstitching, try to pick up only MC-colored stitches so all your whipstitching will be invisible and won't show through the FC of your smaller pieces.

Felting

Now you're ready for felting! There are many ways to go about this—you can research them on the Internet—but here is a basic rundown of one method.

Place your project inside a white zippered pillowcase or tie off a regular white pillowcase with a rubber band. This will protect your washing machine from fiber fuzzies and your project from towel and clothing lint. Put the pillowcase in your machine, and throw in a couple of white towels or very old, light-colored jeans or pants (so no dye will run through the water and affect the color of your project) to aid in agitation. Put in a little bit of laundry detergent and set the water to hot and the size of the load to the smallest possible setting. Some people say to check on your project every five minutes because the felting process is magical and may happen at any given moment—you don't want to overfelt your piece. I end up checking my pieces every fifteen minutes, which is when I have to reset the time on my machine to keep it

agitating and to keep it from rinsing just yet. I find I usually need thirty to thirty-five minutes of agitation for this particular project. Set a timer if you have one.

When you check your project, take it out of the pillow case, squeeze out some water and see if there are still visible stitch holes or if the piece is still really floppy and stretchy. Felting is finished when you feel like your crochet work has become more of a solid fabric. I usually then put it back in the case and just let the machine rinse and spin. Some people rinse felted pieces by hand and press out the water to avoid the possibility of the project getting warped in the rinse cycle. I generally find that nothing horrible happens to my work, and if anything needs to be reshaped by hand, I can still do so while the piece is somewhat wet. Then I leave the project to air-dry completely for one to two days.

6

Here's a photo to give you an idea of how much smaller your project will be once you've finished felting it. I'm always amazed by how much of a difference there is!

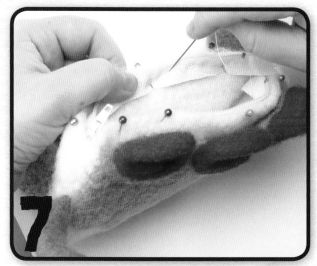

When your pouch is completely dry, sew the zipper between Panel A and B with a needle and thread that matches your MC. Follow the directions on your zipper packaging if you want to shorten the zipper to better fit the length of your pouch opening. I like to place my zipper first with pins to make sewing easier. Then, using matching thread, sew each side of the zipper to its corresponding panel. I use a backstitch. Try to sew as straight and clean and uniform as possible, because your stitches will probably show, even though the thread matches in color.

Now begins the really fun part—decorating your Cake Monster! I use big black buttons for eyes. Remember to only sew through Panel C, or you'll sew all the way through your front pocket! Give your strawberries a cute little sprig of green by tying on small bows of green ribbon. Sew through the center of each bow a little bit to prevent them from untying. Then sew the center of each bow to the base of each strawberry, being careful to sew only through Panel C. If you are worried about the ends of your ribbon bows unraveling, you can quickly pass the ends through a candle. Be careful with very thin ribbon—I find you need to pass the ribbon only near the flame and not actually in it.

At this point, you could be done! But I am personally in the "more is more" camp. For sprinkles, I use mini pom-poms in a rainbow of colors. I use Fabri-Tac, which is permanent and washable, to adhere them. You can use any colors you like, or use seed beads or bugle beads instead. To give my strawberries some seeds, I use five Swarovski crystals on each berry, adhering them with Gem-Tac. You could also use seed beads or bugle beads.

Monster Tip

Another way to keep ribbon ends from fraying is to spread a thin layer of Fabri-Tac over the cut ends.

booger BITER

This tissue-box cover is a nasty little booger. He silently waits in the corner of the room for an unsuspecting snoofty-nosed sickie to come along. He knows how badly you want that soft white thing to relieve your drippy, runny, oozing proboscis. Just as you go to grab one, he chomps! Watch out! In the winter months, it's possible you could see one in every room. They tend to multiply when germs are lingering about. He never fails to lure his prey if loaded with those fancy lotion-coated tissues. You might be better off using a handkerchief.

materials & tools

Tissue box

Two 10½" × 13½" (27cm × 34cm) pieces of plastic canvas

Scissors

One small piece of white plastic canvas

One skein each worsted weight yarn in black, white, orange, purple and green

Tapestry needle

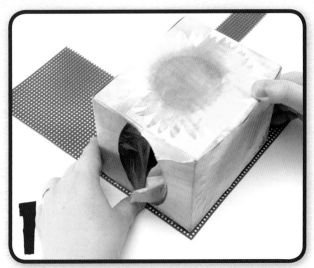

To size the canvas to your own tissue box, lay the canvas against the side of the box, and trim the canvas so it fits the box and has an extra row of holes on the tops and sides but not on the bottom. To size the top, match the number of holes along each edge of the top to the number of holes along the top edge of the corresponding side piece. Two of the sides of the box I used here were each 31 holes wide × 36 holes tall; the other two were 29 × 36. Therefore, the top was 31 × 29.

You'll need four box sides, one box top and six teeth (or the number needed to fit across two sides of tissue opening—see the diagram on page 69). Cut a square section out of the center of the top piece to fit the hole for the tissues (this doesn't have to be too precise). My hole was 21 holes × 17 holes.

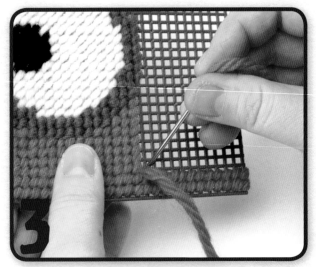

Weave the yarn faces onto the canvas sides. To weave, cut a piece of yarn about 2' (.6m) long. Start from the back and pull up to the front, leaving about a 4" (10cm) tail. Stitch down again through the hole diagonally, next to where you came up. Keep all stitches slanted in the same direction. Do one color at a time. Don't worry about what the back looks like. See the chart on page 69 for the eyes, placing them wherever you'd like on each side. Just be sure that wherever you start, you leave enough canvas holes on all sides to accommodate the design. Once you've finished the chart, fill in the rest of each side with another color yarn.

When you must change colors or you run out of a piece of yarn, weave in your end. Push the needle through, beneath a number of backstitches.

Pull the needle through, and cut the yarn near the canvas. On the side panels, stitch around the edge of one of the short sides (this will be the bottom edge). To do this, sew up through an edge hole, wrap the yarn around the edge to the other side of the canvas and come back up through the next hole. For the top panel, stitch around the inside edges of the hole you cut for the tissue opening.

For the teeth, start by working around one edge of the tooth and then work the middle. Come back to the other edge.

Leave the edge of the jagged row of the tooth unsewn.

Place each tooth, with its jagged edge lined up with one of the long inside edges of the top, where you'd like it to go. Connect the teeth to the top by stitching them together through the holes. Stitch all the way across the top. Weave the yarn back to where the other yarn end is, and tie the two ends together.

Sew the four sides together as you sewed on the teeth, making sure you line up the edge holes of one side with the edge holes of the other.

Sew on the top in the same way. Weave in any remaining loose ends of yarn.

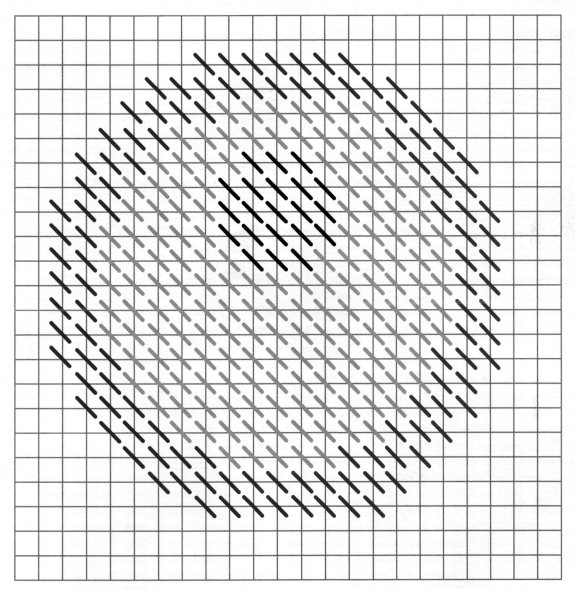

Booger Biter eyeball chart

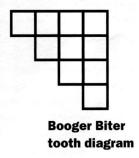

**Booger Biter
tooth diagram**

micro beasts Z2X4-Z6Q3

Little beasts are everywhere. Some of them are so small you can't see them. While a few are quite deadly and serious, others are pretty charming and funny. These little guys are harmless and are actually quite hilarious. If you could hear the jokes they tell, you'd definitely giggle. You'd learn to have a sense of humor like theirs, too, if you had two heads or five legs. Being microscopic isn't all that bad if you learn to make the best of it. Of course, they all secretly wish they could be worthy of causing an epidemic. That has its problems, too, so "be careful what you wish for" is an oft-spoken reminder between Micro Beast pals. Another favorite saying of theirs: "Embrace your cuteness."

materials & tools

Enough black felt for the number of *Micro Beasts* you wish to create

Scissors

Seam ripper

Cotton woven fabric

Embroidery hoop

Safety-lock eyes

Faux-fur scraps

Embroidery needle

Embroidery floss in assorted colors

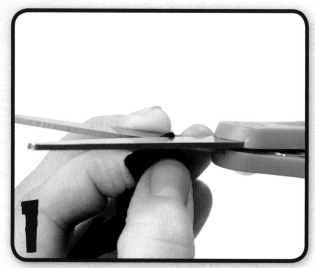

Cut a felt monster. Let your imagination run wild for the shapes—mine tend toward the amoeboid strain of monsterdom. Snip a small hole in the monster where its eye should go by folding the felt snowflake-style and then snipping.

Secure the cotton woven fabric in your embroidery hoop. Use a seam ripper to cut a hole in the cotton woven fabric through which the eye will be inserted. You need only a very small hole, just big enough so you can finagle the post of an eye through. If your hole is too big, the eye will fall out.

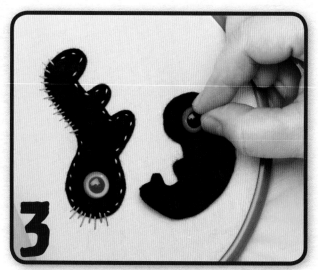

Position the hole in your beast over the hole in the embroidery fabric. Put an eye through both holes.

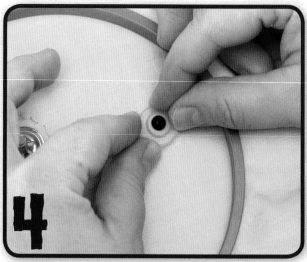

Attach the safety-lock eye's backing to secure the eye in place. Pull the embroidery fabric tight again in the hoop if it has come loose. Repeat Steps 1–4 for as many beasts as you'd like.

5 Using two threads of floss or a single thread doubled up, embroider your beasts. The following steps show some types of stitches I like to use.

Scruffy scraggle stitch: Come up through both fabrics near the monster's edge. Sew back down through the embroidery fabric directly above to make a scraggly hair on the monster.

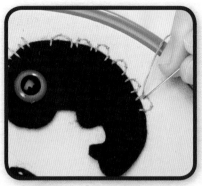

Scaly stitch: Sew up through both fabrics near the edge of your beast. Sew back down through both fabrics a little to one side, but leave a short length of loose thread for a loop. Tack the loop down by making a couple tiny stitches over it.

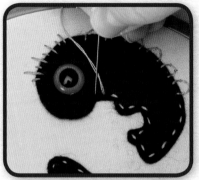

Galumphing stitch: Outline the monster with a running stitch.

Twinkle wart stitch: Make a short stitch. Cross over it with another short stitch in a different direction. Repeat until you have a spiny wart. (I use about four stitches for each of my warts.)

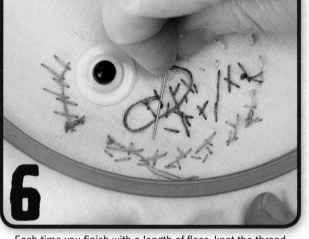

6 Each time you finish with a length of floss, knot the thread and then run the needle under the stitches at the back of the embroidery fabric to secure the tail.

Beard-attaching stitch: Slide a faux-fur scrap underneath the beast at one end to look like a beard. Sew over it, working through both fabrics and the beard, using a backstitch.

CHAPTER 3
BEASTIE BONES

It's a little known fact that monsters in general (and those in this chapter in particular) are big into recycling—paper clips (perfect for fishing out belly-button lint!), fish scales (delicious with a smear of earwax), nose hairs (don't ask).... Nothing goes to waste. As a matter of fact, dumpster diving is one of the monster nation's favorite pastimes, be it for ecominded intentions or for the pure sensory enjoyment of it.

So, in the spirit of repurposing, the following projects explore the beastie makings all around you. That foil takeout tray; that empty (as in, no more Marbits) box of Lucky Charms; that sludge of junk mail that's taken over your kitchen island; bottle caps, wood scraps, stray buttons…it's all fair fodder for monster making. Now you can clean your house and get your creative groove on all in one fell swoop. "Be mean and go green!" as my monsters friends say. (They just love to trash talk.)

the great CHOMPY McChomperson

What lurks inside this creepy old box? Why, it's not a box at all, but rather an old, beat-up, carnival-performing beastly contraption. In its heyday, it used to perform tricks like Hide the Golden Coin and Swallow the Raven. Now it sits rusty and alone, barely even able to lift its tarnished lid. Offer it some assistance, if you will. Open it up and hide a little something inside. It might not even make a creak, but it will secretly rejoice to relive its glory days. Don't get freaked out by all those eyes under the cap—if you stare into them long enough, you will sense the beautiful feeling of overwhelming gratitude this rusty old box has after you've helped it regain a taste of its youth.

materials & tools

Small round cardboard box

Black, metallic silver, brown and red (to match felt) paint

Paintbrush

1 aluminum takeout tray*

Hard rounded or flat object

Tin snips

Sandpaper

Permanent marker

Flat-head screwdriver

Paper towels

Strong craft glue

1 aluminum can*

Small clamps

10" × 5" (25cm × 13cm) red felt*

Scissors

Tacky glue

Googly eyes

*The amount needed for each of these items will depend on the exact dimensions of your box. The numbers given work for my 3" × 1½" (8cm × 4cm) box.

Paint the outside of the box black. Paint a very thin coat of metallic silver paint over the black to give it a dark steel look. Set aside to dry.

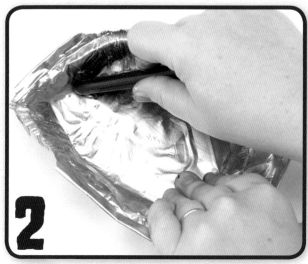

Flatten out an aluminum takeout container with a hard rounded or flat object, such as a closed pocket knife, a pen with a rounded cap or a bone folder. The resulting piece doesn't need to be perfectly smooth, but all the major ridges and bumps should be worked out to create a metal skin.

Using tin snips, cut a circle about ½" (1cm) bigger than your box lid out of the flattened metal. Sand one side of the circle, and paint it with a thin wash of black paint. Let it dry. Use a permanent marker to trace the lid in the center of the circle. Mark where you'd like screws to go.

Using the end of a paintbrush or a similar object with a rounded point, make circular impressions to look like screw heads. Work from the back of the metal (the unpainted side) so that when the metal is flipped right side up, the screws stand out on top. Mark the edges of the screws clearly in the metal, using enough pressure to make the fake screws visible, but being careful not to create any holes. You can always make the impression deeper, but if you cut a hole, you'll have to start over with a new piece of metal.

Use a flat-head screwdriver to make the slots in the screws, this time working on the painted side of the metal and pressing toward the back to make indents. Again, be careful with the amount of pressure you use.

Add some brown paint over the entire piece of metal, leaving extra paint around the edges of the screws and in their slots. Dab the paint off with a paper towel to antique everything a bit.

Lightly sand the edges of the rivets to highlight them.

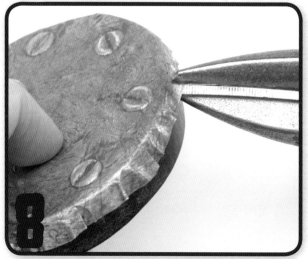

Center the box lid in the circle, with the box top against the unpainted side of the metal, and use your hands to fold the edges of the metal down around the lid. Take the metal off, add strong craft glue and adhere the metal to the box top. Make small snips in the edge of the metal to help fit it to the box lid (this edge will be hidden by another piece of metal). I'm using heavy-duty shears, but you don't need anything that extreme—your tin snips will do.

Open the snips a few at a time. Add a line of glue to the corresponding area on the lid, and glue a section down. Then move on to the next section, continuing around the entire circumference of the lid. Follow Steps 3–9 to make another circle, and fit it to the bottom of the box, skipping the instructions for adding the screws.

Cut two strips for the teeth out of a soda can. To fit my box, I cut strips about 9½" long × ¾" wide (24cm × 2cm). Fashion the strips into rows of teeth. Treat the strips the same way you did the metal circle for the top of the box, by painting, sanding and adding screws to the blank side of the metal. Sand the edges of the teeth to highlight them.

Add some glue to a small section of the edge of the box lid. Adhere one of the strips of teeth, aligning the straight edge of the strip with the top edge of the lid. Clamp the teeth in place. Allow that section to dry before continuing in the same way around the lid, doing one small section at a time. Repeat for the other strip of teeth, adding it to the bottom of the box so that when the box is assembled, the two rows point toward each other.

Monster Tip

Gluing items in sections like this and allowing each section to dry before moving on to the next is a time-consuming process. However, don't skimp on the dry time required by the particular glue you're using, or the box won't be as sturdy. Instead, work on the box for a little while and then find a safe place to leave it to dry where no one will disturb it. Come back later.

12

Paint the inside of the lid the same red color as your felt. If you can't find paint the right color, mix several colors together until you're happy with the result. If I still can't get the color exactly right, I lean toward making the paint darker than the felt so the paint recedes from the eye's attention.

13

Cut two circles of felt to fit inside the top and bottom of your box. Cut a strip to fit around the inside circumference of the box. My strip was 9½" × 1¾" (24cm × 4cm). This gave me a little extra length—so the ends overlapped—and a little extra depth—so the felt continued down the sides of the box and a little onto the bottom, eliminating gaps between it and the felt circle. Tacky glue the felt inside the sides, bottom and lid. Trim the felt as necessary.

14

Use tacky glue to adhere an assortment of googly eyes to the inside of the lid.

Monster Tip

Dust off your high school math skills when it comes time to figure out the length of material you'll need to fit around the circumference of a circular object. Multiply the diameter of the circle by π (3.14). Of course, if you have a flexible tape measure, use that!

the all-seeing CUBES OF chance

Would you care or do you dare to play a game of chance? Roll the die—or roll two or three dice. How many eyes do you see? All those eyes see you as well. For every eye that lands facing the sky, a secret hidden deep within your soul will be released. Play the game alone, and discover your innermost desires yet unknown. Play with friends, and your true selves will be revealed to each other. Play with enemies for the ultimate challenge of "can you handle the truth?" Be warned—if you act silly while playing with these dice, they will only reveal your most ridiculous truths and intentions. If you wear a name tag with the wrong name while rolling, you might get the wrong truths. If you use them to play board games, their sacred intuition might be squashed for all eternity. (In that case, you could always make some more.)

materials & tools

Scissors

Cardboard cereal box

Glossy acrylic decoupage medium

Craft knife

Craft glue

Pin

Decorative papers

Black, brown and gold acrylic paint

Paintbrush

Pencil

Circle template

Black construction paper

Tacky glue

21 googly eyes*

Ruler

*To make a proper, usable game die, you'll need to put a different number of eyes on each side of the cube (1, 2, 3, 4, 5 and 6). The eyes for the sides with larger numbers should be small enough to all fit on the same die face. The eyes for smaller numbers can be larger.

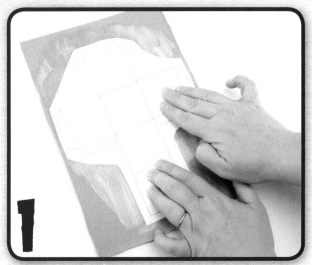

Enlarge the template on page 87, and use decoupage medium to adhere it to the cereal box.

Cut the cereal box along the outer lines of the template using a craft knife. Score along the interior lines by cutting only partway through the box, or use the back side of the knife blade.

Add craft glue to all the tabs created by the scored lines, and form the template into a cube. Gluing the final side in place can be tricky because you can't get your finger inside to press the tabs. I like to insert a pin in the corners near those final tabs to press them against the side of the cube from the inside.

Cut decorative papers to fit each side of the cube. Glue them in place.

Monster Tip

When I'm gluing items like decorative papers that I don't want to get messy, I use a scrap of paper or cardboard to spread the glue evenly over the item before laying it in place. This keeps my fingers free from glue and prevents large globs of glue from oozing out around the edges.

5

Brush black paint lightly onto the edges of the six sides to give them a slightly aged look. Be careful where you place your fingers as you do this—you don't want to leave black fingerprints everywhere! Allow the paint to dry thoroughly.

6

Cover all sides of the cube with the decoupage medium. Brush the medium right over and around the edges of the cube, sealing them shut.

7

Use the decoupage medium to adhere a piece of decorative paper onto a strip of the cereal box. Design a monster face for that side of the cube and trace it onto the paper. Cut out the shape. Make six faces, using a different paper and shape for each face. Make sure each face is small enough to fit on one side of the cube but large enough to accommodate the correct number of googly eyes.

8

Lightly paint the edges of each face with brown paint, followed by gold, to antique them.

Place the faces onto the sides of the cube, and paint a wash of decoupage medium over them to adhere them in place.

Trace black construction paper circles a little larger than your googly eyes. Trace slightly larger circles around the first circles.

Use the two circles as a guide to make zigzag cuts for the monster eyelashes.

Place the eyelashes on the die faces, and cover with a wash of decoupage medium. Use tacky glue to glue the googly eyes onto the eyelashes.

**The All-Seeing Cubes
of Chance template**
Reproduce at 100%

freaky FIENDY monsters

Sometimes gunk and funk just pile up and up. Your mailbox provides a never-ending supply of junk: The credit card offers keep coming, all those party invitations are creating messes, and you've got more messes than dresses! Luckily, if you know the secret, you can synergize that papery mess into an army of fiends that will transmogrify your house (apartment, hobbit hole, whatever) into a stronghold. The more monsters you make, the more power you will have to combat the junky gunky funk! Hang them in your entryway. Gather four, fourteen or more. These scary guys are all on your side. They will shoo the junk away. Shoo! It would also help if you got yourself a recycling bin.

materials & tools

- Polymer clay
- Sandpaper
- Acrylic gloss paint or spray
- Paintbrush
- Wax paper
- Liquid latex
- Junk mail
- Old blender
- Water
- Cup
- Old towels
- Drying rack
- Acrylic paint in white and other assorted colors
- String
- Scissors
- Hot-glue gun

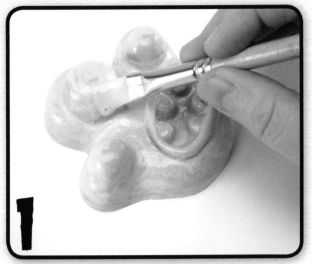

Condition your clay first by rolling it into a snake shape between your hands. Fold it in half and roll it into a snake again. Continue to do this until the clay is soft and doesn't crack when it's folded. Sculpt a monster face from polymer clay. Bake the clay face according to the manufacturer's instructions. Sand the sculpture. Seal with an acrylic gloss paint or spray.

Lay wax paper beneath the sculpture, and paint on a layer of liquid latex. Try not to leave any nooks or crannies uncovered or unfilled. Let the latex dry.

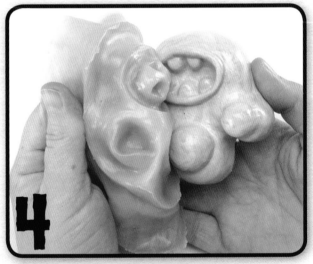

Continue to build layers of latex, letting each layer dry thoroughly before applying the next.

Once you've completed enough latex layers to create a durable mold, peel the finished mold off the sculpture.

Monster Tip

Don't let latex dry in the bristles of your paintbrush, or the brush will be ruined. Wash the paintbrush with clean water each time you're done painting.

Fill an old blender with paper scraps and water. (Once you've used a blender to make paper, designate it for that purpose; don't use it again for food.) The exact ratio of water to paper doesn't matter, but you need enough water to get the paper truly wet and pulpy. I like to use all sorts of junk mail to make my monsters. It seems like a fitting end for such annoyances. Let the mixture soak for thirty minutes.

Puree the paper and water in your blender. Continue blending until you have a fairly uniform, pulpy mush.

Place the mold in a cup or other item so it will stay level and stable. Pour a small amount of the paper pulp into the mold.

Press the water out of the pulp with a towel. Use an old towel you don't mind getting messy, because the ink from the junk mail could stain it.

9

Continue to add pulp and press out the water until the mold is completely full.

10

Release the mush from the mold. You may need to press on the mold to get the monster face out. Try not to press on the smaller details, as these will be more challenging to reshape.

11

Reshape the face a little with your fingers, fixing any spots your fingers marred when you were taking the face out of its mold. Repeat Steps 7–11 to make as many monster faces with the same mold as you like. Blend more paper pulp as necessary.

Monster Tip

The exact color of junk-mail paper pulp varies with every new batch you make. For this project, that's not a problem, because you end up completely concealing the pulp with paint. However, if for some reason you want all your pulp to be the same color, don't use junk mail. Instead, use plain white paper, or find some other paper that is more uniform in appearance and in amount of ink.

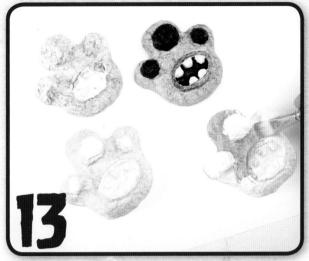

Allow the monster faces to air dry on a rack. The amount of pulp you were able to squeeze into each face will make a difference in its final appearance. I packed the face on the left of this picture very tightly with paper pulp. The face on the right I left a little looser. Neither result is "correct"—it's simply an aesthetic choice.

Paint the monsters white and let them dry. Paint the details of the faces with whatever colors you choose. I picked fluorescents to make my fiends super garish.

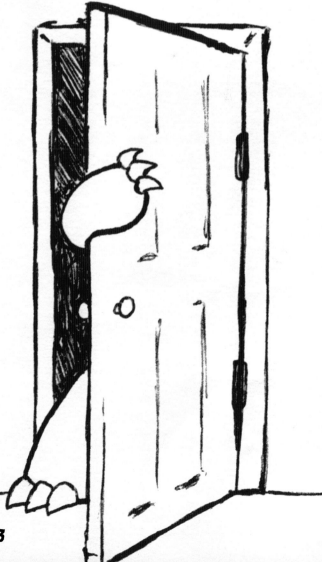

If you want to hang your monsters, glue a loop of string to the backs with a hot-glue gun.

the corky CREW

by Margot Potter

We all love champagne—it's true—but those pesky corks start accumulating, and what's a human to do? Well, if you hide them in a blue box in a cave in Peru for sixty years and sixty days, some jaunty monsters will grow, that's what! Their corky little bodies will attract doodads and ding-a-lings, and their family will multiply. Then they can come back and live with you if you build them a happy home. Set them up on your mantel and play with them every day. Then hide away another boxful, and by the time you're one hundred and twenty, you will have so many cork-monster friends, you won't know what to do! What are you waiting for? Drink up, buttercup!

materials & tools

Champagne cork

Silver metallic, red and glitter paint

Paintbrush

Liquid Fusion glue

2 googly eyes

Wired tinsel

Wire cutters

Pin

Vintage bottle cap

Sharp, pointed object or electric drill

6mm vintage moonglow Lucite bead

Tim Holtz game spinner

Silver-plated headpin

Craft glue

18- and 26-gauge craft wire

Round-nose pliers

Chain-nose pliers

Vintage button

*The above materials are those needed to create Corky, Jr. (on right in photo). See notes on page 97 for more on Mrs. Fizzy (center) and Ginger (left).

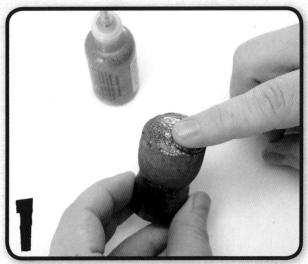

1 Paint the bottom half of a champagne cork silver and the top part red. Use your fingertips to spread a thin layer of glitter paint all over the head on top of the red paint. Allow the paint to dry.

2 Use Liquid Fusion glue to adhere googly eyes to your painted cork. Make sure you place the eyes far enough down on the face so a bottle-cap hat can be added later. Allow the glue to dry.

3 Tie a small amount of tinsel around the neck of your painted cork. Use wire cutters to trim off most of the excess and tuck the tails under in the back.

4 Use a pin to mark the center point of a bottle cap, and drill or poke a hole in it using a sharp, pointed object or an electric drill.

5 Use a headpin to slide a bead, a spinner and your drilled bottle cap on top of your cork head. You may need to cut the headpin shorter depending on the size you have—they can be tough to push into the cork. Dab a little craft glue on the end of the pin before inserting it.

6 Using round-nose pliers, cut off two 1½" (4cm) segments of 18-gauge wire and create arms, looping one end of each wire for a hand.

7 Dab a little glue on the unlooped end of one wire segment. Use the chain-nose pliers to insert the arm into the side of the cork. Gently bend the arm. Repeat for the other arm.

8 Glue a button to the front of the cork. Cut off and insert a small *U*-shaped segment of 26-gauge wire into two holes of the button to secure it.

To make Mrs. Fizzy, follow the same process as for Corky, Jr., but make longer arms and adhere a bottle cap to the bottom of the cork to make her taller. Glue acrylic fun fur under her tilted hat, and add a Tim Holtz metal flower.

To make Corky's friend Ginger, skip the arms, tinsel and bottle caps altogether, and adorn her fun-fur hair with a Tim Holtz metal flower. Stick an extra googly eye in the middle of the flower for good measure. Add facial features with puff paint. Finally, paint her a lovely outfit instead of giving her a decorative button in front.

shimgraloo SHOCKER

By now you may think you know all you need to know about monsters. You may think you've got the skills to save yourself from a sneak attack. And just when you think you're safe, you pull the string on this wooden beast—he seems quite unassuming. You expect him to move into hug position (a hug would be nice right about now). There is no way you could ever be prepared for ferocious teethy arms! You run and hide, but there is no escape. You are compelled to come back and pull the string again and again, despite the horror. Well, really, they're just silly—not so horrific, actually. Hey, those are some funny teeth this monster has! You can forget about the hug, though.

materials & tools

Pencil

7" × 6½" (18cm × 17cm) craft plywood

Small hacksaw or scroll saw

Sandpaper

Drill with ¹⁄₁₆" (2mm) drill bit

Thick piece of wood

Wood glue

Small clamps

Paper clips

Round-nose pliers

Blue, pink, white and pearlescent white acrylic paint

Paintbrush

Acrylic gloss paint

String

Scissors

Hot-glue gun

Wire cutters

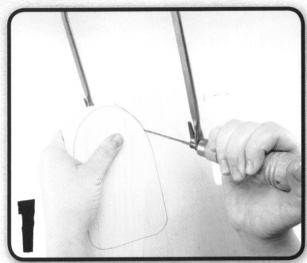

Enlarge the templates on page 104, and trace them onto your wood. You'll need two of each main piece plus eight spacers—two for each position indicated on the body template. Do not cut the spacers out of the body itself—they are there to indicate placement only. Instead, trace them elsewhere onto the wood as separate elements. Use a saw to cut out the wooden pieces.

Sand the edges of the pieces. Make sure you get into all the nooks and crannies on the arms to avoid the pain of splinters later.

Drill holes, with a 1/16" (2mm) drill bit, where indicated on the templates. Put a thick piece of wood behind your monster pieces as you drill to avoid making holes in your work surface.

On each spot indicated on the body template, glue a pair of spacers to one body piece. One spacer should be glued on top of the other. Hold them in place with clamps until they dry.

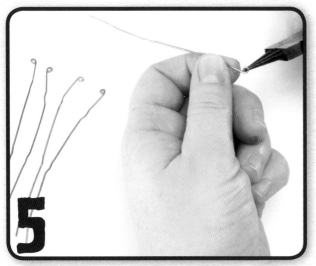

5 Unbend five paper clips, and curl the ends with round-nose pliers. You'll use these to pin together all the wooden elements through the holes you drilled.

6 Paint a thin wash of blue on one side and on the edges of each arm and leg, as well as on the edges of the body piece that does not have the spacers attached. Let the pieces dry. Paint the eyes, teeth and toenails, allowing the paint to dry between each color application. Add a gloss coat over the details to emphasize them. (If you're not going to hang up your monster and would like him to appear at his best from all sides, paint both sides of the arms and legs and the second body piece on the side that doesn't have the spacers.)

7 Push the paper clips up from the back of the body piece that has the spacers through the holes you drilled in Step 3.

Monster Tip

Don't let acrylic paint dry in the bristles of your brush, or the brush will be ruined. Wash out your brush with clean water after each application of paint.

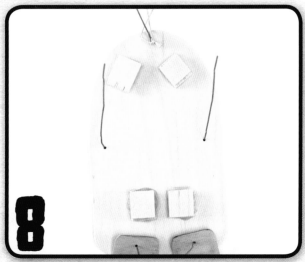

Add the legs by sliding the hole in each leg down over the proper paper clip. Add a loop of string around the paper clip at the top of the monster's head if you want to be able to hang it up.

Tie a string through the top hole of one of the arms. Tie the other end of the string to the top hole in the other arm. Use the distance between the arm paper clips to measure how much string to leave between the arms. Trim the ends of the string.

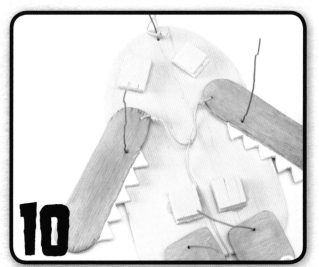

Slide the remaining holes in the arms down over the proper paper clips on the body. Tie another string to the middle of the string strung between the arms. String it down to the base of the monster, passing between the lower spacers and then the leg paper clips. When the monster is finished and you pull on this string, his arms will rise up, revealing his hidden teeth!

Monster Tip

If you're worried that your knots may come untied, simply add a dab of liquid glue to each, allowing it to dry before moving on.

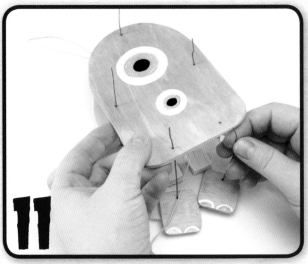

Position the top painted piece over the assembled parts, and push it down, fitting the paper clips through the holes.

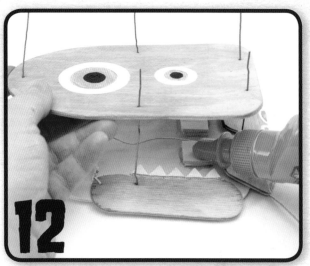

With a hot-glue gun, apply glue to the top of the spacers. Align the body pieces, and clamp them together while the glue dries.

Using pliers, make loops with the wire ends in the front.

Pull the length of the wires to the back. Using wire cutters, cut them close to the back, and curl them in to secure them in place. Work one wire at a time.

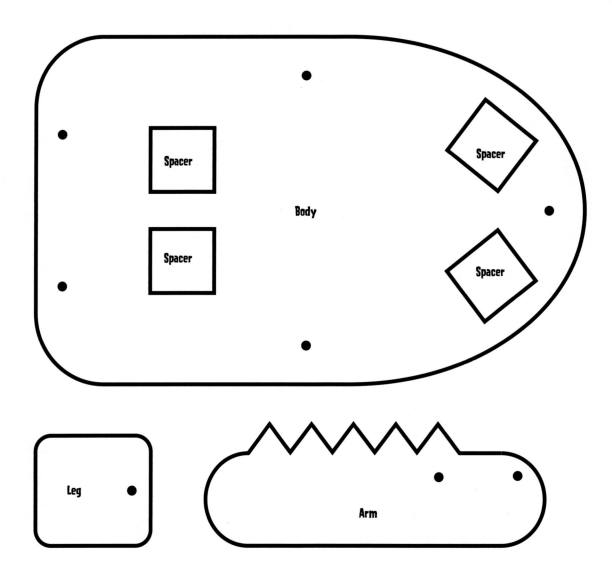

Shimgraloo Shocker templates
Reproduce at 100%

SAVAGE GOONHEADS

by DAVE SAVAGE

The youngest of the Milwaukee Goonheads (direct descendents of the Hungarian clan), Spike and Sally Goonhead do not play well with others. It must be mealtime because Spike is wielding his supersharp fork, and Sally looks ready to dig into her Barbie. You may want to wear eye protection when you pull their strings—Spike's been known to poke more than food with his fork. Ouchie! Hey, I don't know about you, but those cutesy little shirts give me the supercreeps!

Mommy's Little Snuggle Bunny

Instructions

Put me together like this:
Make a color copy of me as huge or as tiny as you like. Be careful cutting me out! Use five brads to attach my appendages where you see the small circles on my parts.

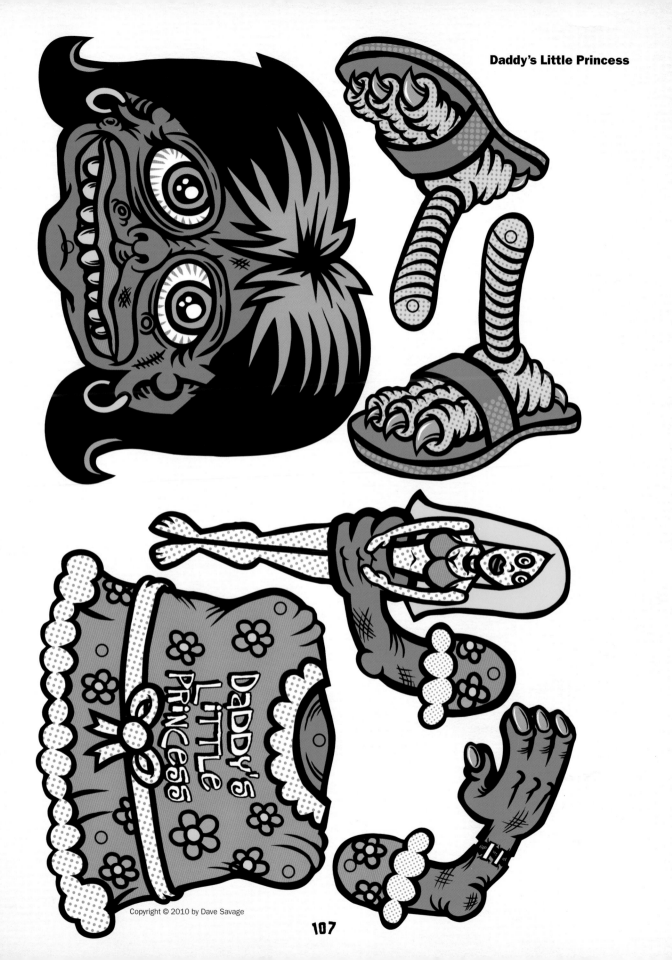

CHAPTER 4

MONSTER MISHMASH

I have saved the most disturbing for last. You may call them outcasts, loners, weirdos—I call them projects-that-just-don't-fit-neatly-into-any-other-chapter. Shunned to the outskirts of monster society, these one-antlered, one-eyed, baby-doll-headed freaks of nature are made of a bit of this, a scrap of that—acrylic paint, stockings, jersey fabric, air-dry clay, rhinestones and other miscellany.

Not very pleasant monsters, this lot. Downright troublesome, actually. As they are without any friends, family or support network, I suppose it's no wonder they've run quite amok, rummaging through your belongings, delivering tickles attributed to bed bugs (HA! you wish) and giving you the heebie-jeebies with their incessant stares. For the record, they hate that "Monster Mash" song. They find it offensive—I found out the hard way. Don't make the same mistake.

Zzyzx the SNEAK

By day, Zzyzx the Sneak adorns your mantel or curio shelf and charms your house guests with its whimsical nature, but by night, he comes to life and roams the house! He is very curious and loves to rummage through the belongings of your guests. He has also been known to crawl under the covers and tickle those temporary inhabitants of the household—especially cousins who have traveled from long distances. He always gets away with it because in the morning the mayhem is chalked up to weird dreams due to sleeping in an unusual place.

materials & tools

Aluminum foil

4–8 oz. polymer clay

Metal ruler

Sandpaper

Acrylic paint in assorted colors

Paintbrush

Pencil or fabric marker

Scissors

10" × 11" (25cm × 28cm) purple faux fur

6" × 6" (15cm × 15cm) blue fuzzy felt

6½" × 10½" (17cm × 27cm) striped jersey shirt fabric

Sewing needle

Strong matching thread

4" × 4" (10cm × 10cm) corrugated cardboard

Glue

Sewing machine (optional)

Pins

Plastic weighted pellets

Old stocking

Polyester fiberfil

Make a tinfoil ball a little smaller than you want the final head of the monster to be. Condition your clay (see Step 1 on page 90 for more information) and then cover the tinfoil ball with it.

Add details to the head with clay—a neck, horns, eyes, a nose and anything else that suits your fancy. To match the body template on page 116, the circumference of the neck should be approximately 5" (13cm).

Monster Tip

You can create funky monster-hide textures in polymer clay fairly easily. Imprint the clay with scales using plastic mesh, score ridges in it with a comb, or press it with a pair of jeans for a truly tough hide. Let your fiendish imagination run wind!

To make a groove for the string that will later attach the head to the fabric body, use a metal ruler to score a ring around the neck.

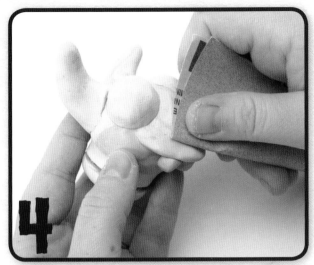

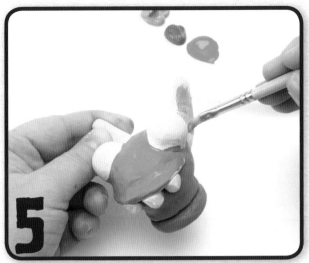

Bake the head according to the manufacturer's instructions. Sand the head to smooth out its texture (unless you like the texture you've arrived at). Rinse off the clay dust under a faucet, and let the piece dry.

Paint the head of the statuette. I gave my head a mottled look by applying an uneven wash of purple over everything but the eyes and teeth. I added green to the rims of the bugged-out eyes, plus a metallic sheen to the monster's horns.

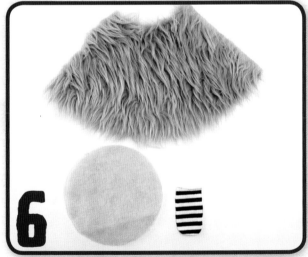

Cut out all your fabric pieces (see the templates on page 116). You'll need one each of the body and felt-wrap pieces, plus twelve arm pieces. When cutting out the arm pieces, cut one first and then carefully line up its stripes with the fabric; trace around it so the second arm matches. Make six pairs in this way.

Handsew a straight stitch around the edge of the felt circle about ¼" (6mm) in. Leave the two ends of the thread loose, with a little extra on each end.

Cut out two circles from the cardboard for the bottom of the statuette (see the template on page 116). Glue the two circles together and allow to dry. Place the cardboard circle inside the felt circle. Pull the thread ends to gather the fabric around the cardboard. Tie the threads in a knot to secure the gathers.

Fold the body fabric in half, and pin the long straight edges of the fur fabric right sides together, carefully tucking in the fur fibers. Sew the fur along the pinned edge using about a ¼" (1cm) seam allowance.

Pin the pairs of arm pieces right sides together along the curved edge, leaving the bottom straight edge open. Sew along the pinned edges using about a ¼" (1cm) seam allowance.

Cut small snips into the seam allowance of each arm piece, and trim it back some. This will help you turn and stuff the arms properly.

Turn all the arms right side out; use a pen or pencil to do this if necessary. (Be sure the pen is capped—you don't want the ink to bleed through!)

Insert the clay head into the furry body (fur on the inside) through the larger opening in the tube, neck first. The bottom of the neck should stick out the small hole at one end of the fur. Sew a straight stitch around the neck. Pull both ends of the thread to draw it closed, fitting the string into the groove you made in the neck. Tie a knot to secure.

Turn the monster right side out. Pour the plastic pellets into the stocking, and tie it shut. It should be about the size of a small apple. Stuff the monster with polyester fiberfil. Place the bag of pellets on top.

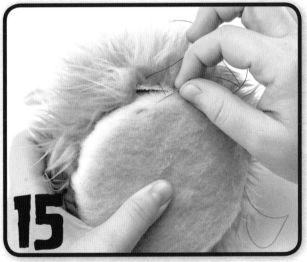

Place the felt-covered cardboard bottom over the pellet pouch and sew it in place with a ladder stitch.

Stuff the arms and sew each one shut. Pin the arm to the body, catching the fur, and then catching the arm, and then catching more fur. Use two pins, one on each side of the arm.

With the arms held securely in place by the pins, sew the arms onto the body, stitching all the way around the circumference of each arm.

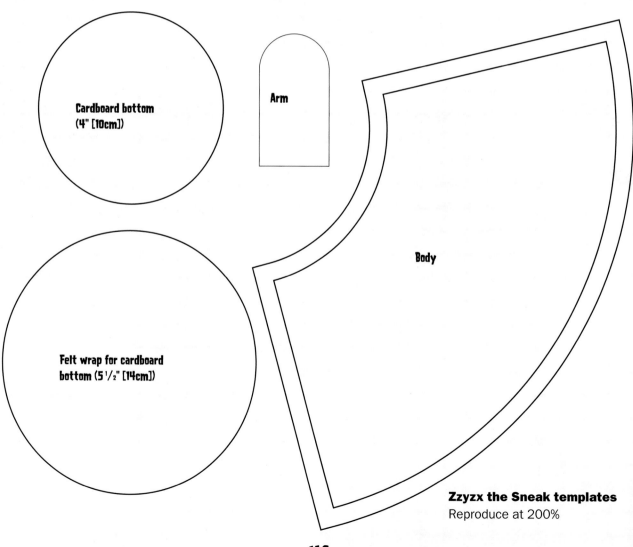

Cardboard bottom
(4" [10cm])

Arm

Body

Felt wrap for cardboard
bottom (5 1/2" [14cm])

Zzyzx the Sneak templates
Reproduce at 200%

WTHP THE LISP

by Leslie Levings

Zzyzx's first cousin twice removed, *Wthp the Lisp*, likes to spend his nights wthpering long, spittly words in sleeping ears ("Sthuccotash," "sthupersthithious," "intesthtinal disthcomfort"). Icky-ew! Gives me the willies just thinking about it. *Wthp* was recently downsized after many dedicated years of working the Spook-A-Rama haunted house in Coney Island. Management cited his increasingly obsessive resentment ever since the pompadour went out of style. Truly, he hasn't been the same since.

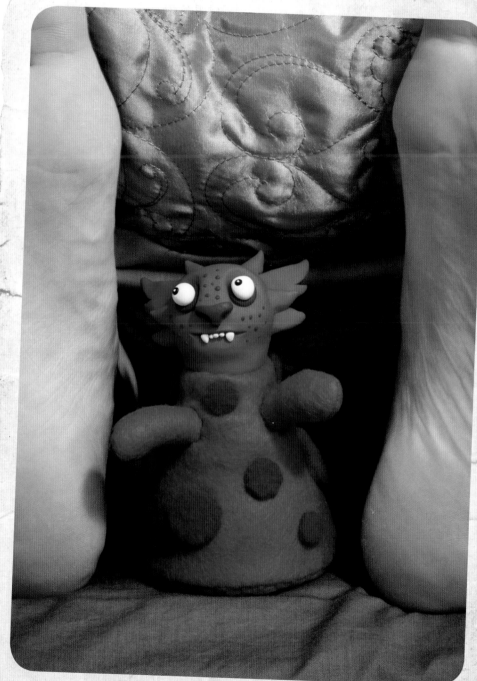

eyeballs, eyeballs EVERYWHERE!

Every inanimate object secretly wants a pair of eyes. Some objects are greedy and want three or more. You can make friends with your garbage can, paper shredder and lamp by supplying them with creepy eyes they can use to stare at you. Have fun with all your new friends! On the other hand, be careful not to give sight to too many of your belongings, or you may arrive home to an empty house!

materials & tools

Round measuring spoon

Lightweight air-dry clay

Acrylic paint

Paintbrush

Acrylic gloss paint

Craft glue

Faux-fur scraps

Magnets, shank buttons, hook-and-loop fasteners or double-stick foam tape

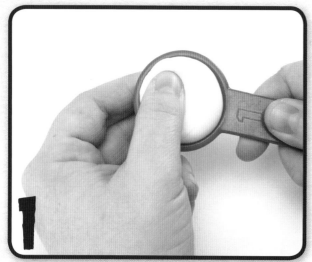

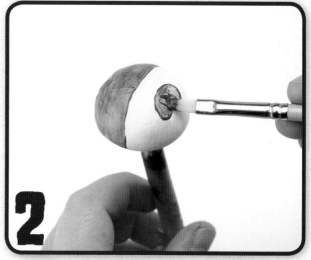

Use a round-bowled measuring spoon to mold eyeballs out of lightweight air-dry clay (I used a tablespoon). Pop them out carefully, reshaping any flaws created in the process. Let the clay dry.

Paint the eyeball as desired. Add a layer of gloss.

Use craft glue to attach dimensional elements, such as strips of fun fur for eyelashes.

Glue hook-and-loop fasteners, buttons, double-stick foam tape or magnets to the back of each eyeball. If you use buttons, make sure not to glue all the way to the edges, or you won't be able to use them in button holes.

Monster Tip

Designate your measuring spoon as your eyeball spoon and don't use it again for food.

CUFF WINKS

by Moxie

Ever wonder what happens to all the eyes that get poked out with icicles, BB guns and the like? They sprout pointy and clippy parts and become fashion accessories—suitable only for those with an odd sense of style and the resolve to withstand the feeling of being constantly watched. It also helps to be able to laugh indulgently at predictable jokes about giving someone the evil eye. Do not—are you listening to me?—do *not* get into a staring contest with these eyes. You will probably lose.

the amulet of BEASTLY peace

In a land where nothing is sacred, one fine young beast shall rise up and summon order and peace among all monsters. It has been foreseen, and so it is written. The power shall come from an amulet forged by her own claws. It will possess a mighty balance of glamour and scariness. Above all else, it will look fabulous with her outfit.

materials & tools

No. 6 plastic food containers

Craft knife

Sandpaper

Pencil

Paper

Single-hole punch

Green and silver pearlescent acrylic paint

Paintbrush

Towel

Permanent marker

Craft heat tool

Awl or other pointy object

Wood block

8 small jump rings

Jeweler's pliers

Jewel glue

3 blue flat-back rhinestones

Find some clear plastic food containers with recycling number 6 on the back. Using a craft knife, cut out some flat pieces, and sand them to a frosted finish.

Rinse and dry the plastic to get rid of the plastic dust. Draw head, jaw and leg designs for your amulet on paper, and trace the designs onto the prepared plastic. Remember, you'll be shrinking these designs, so make them larger than your planned result. Not every piece of plastic will shrink the same amount or in the same way—it may shrink unevenly, so be open to experimenting. As a rough estimate, the designs will shrink to about a third of their original size. Plan where you'd like the holes for the jump rings to make sure you have enough room for them all. Remember, the space between them will shrink, too. Include holes to attach the jaw to the head and two holes at the top of the head.

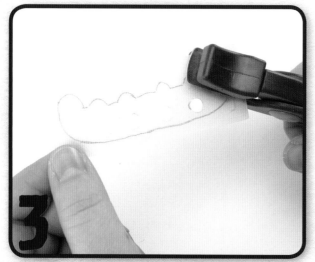

Cut the plastic pieces apart near the traced lines, but don't cut out their detailed shapes yet. (Cut in toward the center of the plastic rather than along straight lines parallel to the edges—otherwise, the plastic may break.) Punch holes in the pieces where you've indicated. Cut the pieces out the rest of the way. Sand the holes and edges of the pieces to make them smooth.

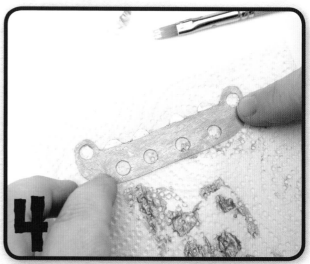

Paint both sides of all the pieces as desired (I used silver and green pearlescent liquid acrylic that's more like ink than paint). Using a towel, dab the paint off the painted pieces. What you're aiming for is more of a stain than a real paint layer. The colors will become more saturated and vibrant as the plastic shrinks. Paint the smaller details, and dab again.

Draw graphic details on the legs with a permanent marker.

Use a craft heat tool to shrink the plastic. I like to use an awl or other pointy object to hold the plastic in place under the heat as it shrinks. Plastic from different containers will shrink differently. Typically, the pieces will curl up and then flatten out as they shrink. If the plastic piece is not perfectly flat after heating, use a wood block to flatten it before it cools completely.

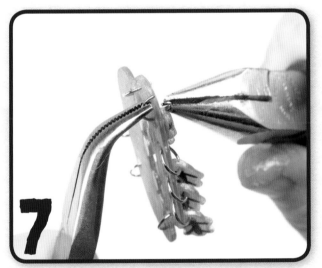

Use jump rings and small jeweler's pliers to attach the head and jaw pieces together and to attach the feet to the jaw. Insert two jump rings in the holes at the top of the head. You can pass the chain of a necklace through these.

Glue on the rhinestone eyes with jewel glue.

Monster Tip

To open a jump ring, hold a set of pliers in each hand. Grip one end of the ring in each pliers and rotate one end towards you. Do not open by pulling the ends directly away from each other. This will change the form of the ring and weaken it.

the fantastic BABY snarky-lark

No monster maker's repertoire would be complete without a couple creepy baby-doll heads thrown into the mix. Why do I think baby heads are creepy? I don't know! Do you think they're creepy? How about when done up with a big glittery antler and fuzzy hair on a faux-bois plaque? You can't wait to hang this up on your parlor wall and tell all your friends about how you lured the creature into your snare through a duel of wits. Do you think they will believe you when you say, "Should've seen the one that got away!"?

materials & tools

- 4 pieces of 8" × 8" (20cm × 20cm) corrugated cardboard
- Craft glue
- Pencil
- Small hacksaw or scroll saw
- White, tan, dark brown and chartreuse acrylic paint
- Paintbrush
- Circle template
- Drill with 1/16" (2mm) drill bit
- Wood block
- Bendable wire
- Wire cutters
- Lightweight air-dry clay
- Dark blue and light blue glitter paint
- Fabric marker
- Scissors
- 8½" × 9½" (22cm × 24cm) pink faux fur
- Pins
- Sewing machine (optional)
- Strong sewing needle (such as a doll needle)
- Strong matching thread
- Vinyl doll head
- Craft knife
- Thimble
- Hot-glue gun
- Polyester fiberfill
- Pom-poms
- Picture hanger

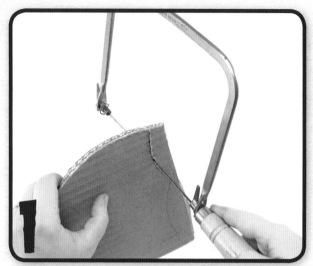

Glue three or four pieces of cardboard together. Enlarge the backboard template on page 135, and trace onto the cardboard. Cut out the backboard with a hacksaw or anything else that will cut through the layers.

Paint a layer of white on one side and on the edges of the board. Let the paint dry.

Paint a layer of dark brown paint on top of the white. Add some water to thin it out a bit as you brush. The intent is to create a finish that looks something like a piece of wood, so you don't want the color to be completely uniform. Let the paint dry.

Apply the tan paint in a wood-grain design. Make sure you continue the grain down over the edges of the board. Let the paint dry.

5

Paint a wash of dark brown over the tan grain, allowing the grain to show through. Let the paint dry.

6

Trace a 2¾" (7cm) circle in the center of the backboard, with the top of the circle about 1¾" (4cm) down from the tip of the center peak.

7

Drill holes around the circle every ¼" (6mm) with a 1/16" (2mm) drill bit. Place a block of wood beneath your cardboard as you drill to avoid making holes in your work surface.

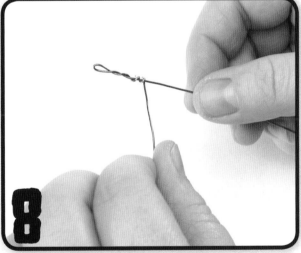

8

Make two antlers out of wire, each approximately 5" (13cm) long (see the template on page 135). To begin, pull out a 6" (15cm) length of wire, and with the wire still attached to the spool, fold the wire back on itself. Wrap the wire around itself back to the other end.

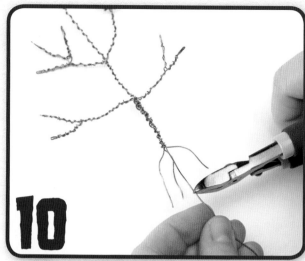

Continue, creating the first two branches by wrapping the wire off to the side and then back down on itself toward the trunk, leaving the final 1" (3cm) unwrapped. When you're down to the base, cut the wire from the spool, leaving another 1" (3cm) of extra wire.

Make more branches by starting a new run of wire off to the side at an angle and wrapping the same way you did for the main trunk in Step 9. The branches don't need to look that nice, because they will be covered with clay. Using the wire cutters, snip off the wire ends. Start another piece of wire, and, leaving 1" (3cm) of wire at the base, wrap all the way up the main trunk of the antler and back down again. Cut the wire, leaving 1" (3cm) of extra wire.

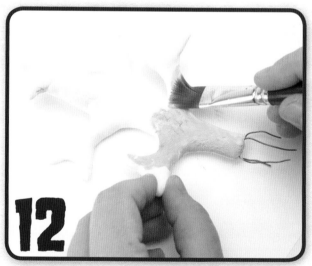

Using lightweight air-dry clay, cover the wire antler. Make sure the four 1" (3cm) wire ends poke out of the bottom at four different angles.

Paint the clay chartreuse. Let the paint dry.

13 Brush on several layers of dark blue glitter paint, followed by several layers of ice blue, allowing each paint layer to dry before adding the next.

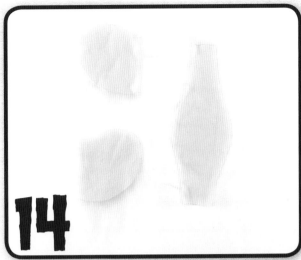

14 Cut out the remaining pattern pieces (see the templates on page 135). You'll need one main head strip and two head sides. Flip the template over before tracing the second head side so you end up with mirror-image pieces.

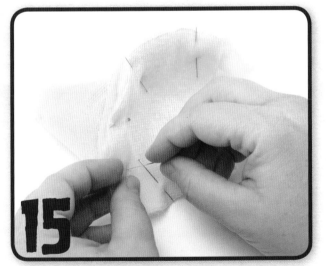

15 Pin the left head side to the main head strip, right sides together, matching point *A* to point *A*, and point *B* to point *B*. Pin one end first and then the other end, and then pin the rest of the edge together, easing it in place as you go.

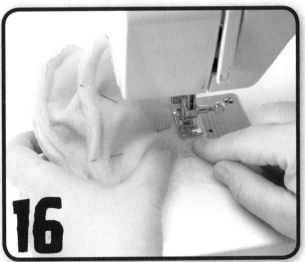

16 Sew along the pinned edges using about a ¼" seam allowance.

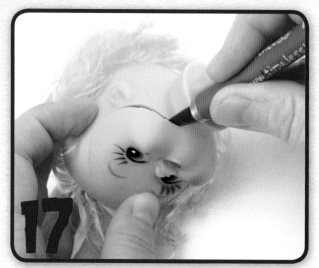

Using a craft knife, cut the doll's face from the head.

With the sewn head piece still inside out, mark the placement of the face. Place the face at the center of the widest part of the main head strip and trace.

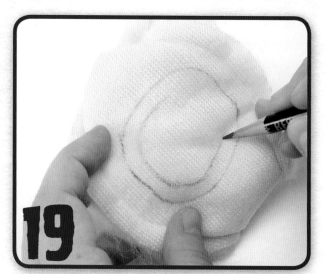

Trace another line ¼" (6mm) inside the one you traced.

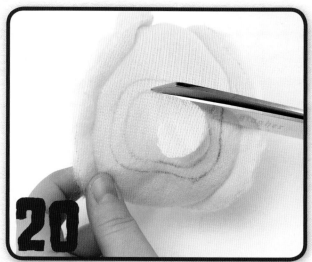

Use scissors to cut out the inner circle (see Tip on page 16 for information about cutting fur).

21

Mark the middle of the top and of the bottom of the hole you cut in Step 20, and mark the middle of the top and of the bottom of the face for alignment.

22

Place the face (facing in) inside the hole, and handsew it in place, using the Step 21 marks as guides. Check it every few stitches to make sure it's not puckering and that the marks line up, and ease it back into place. Use a thimble to help push the needle through the face. You'll need a strong needle such as a doll needle to push through the material.

23

Turn the head right side out. Stick the four wire ends of the antler into the top of the head and through the fabric.

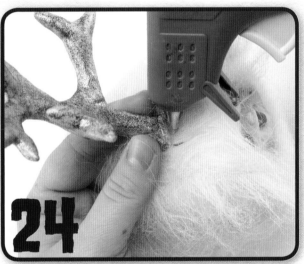

24

Apply a glob of hot glue under the antler before you push it all the way onto the head.

133

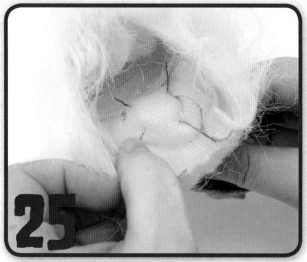

Splay the four ends of wire inside the head to anchor it. Hold the pieces in place until the glue is cool.

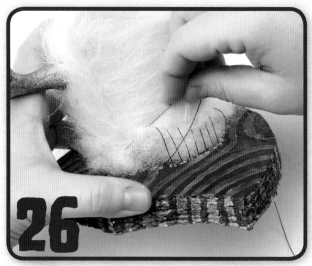

Stuff the head. Sew the head to the board through the holes you drilled in Step 7, starting from the back. Pull tight as you go.

Glue the pom-poms to the side of the head. It helps to spread the pom-pom fibers, apply a dot of glue and then part the hair when attaching each to the head.

Glue a picture hanger to the back of the backboard.

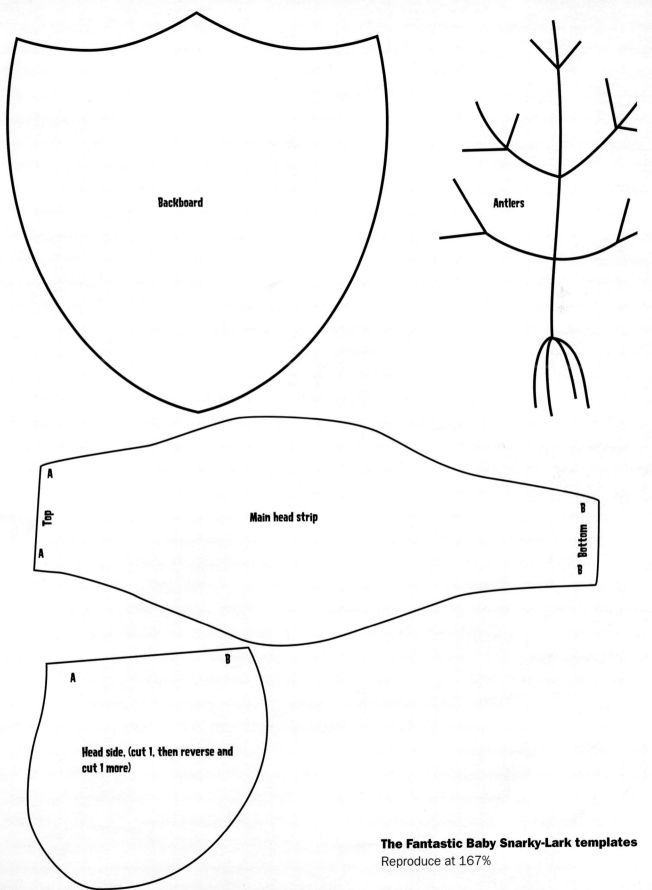

Backboard

Antlers

A

Top

A

Main head strip

B

Bottom

B

B

A

Head side, (cut 1, then reverse and cut 1 more)

The Fantastic Baby Snarky-Lark templates
Reproduce at 167%

CONCLUSION

HONK IF YOU LOVE MONSTERS!

But then roll up your windows, and quick! Car honks (and bobble-heads) are known to attract Shugabillies, a nomadic tribe of monsters infamous for wreaking havoc on automobiles. (If your *check engine* light is on, you may be dealing with a Shugabilly infestation.)

For the projects in this book, I've tried to focus on the less troublesome monsters. Even so, I feel obligated to offer a few cautionary notes: Your beasties will, on occasion, emit unholy smells and blame them on you. Sometimes they like to utter words that sound nasty—but aren't really ("Frappé!" "Super duty!"). And, if left unsupervised in your kitchen, they may drop nasty things in your food when you're not looking.

On the bright side, filling your home with these (relatively) docile monsterkinds will help discourage the nastier types from lurking about. Evidence of resident monsters includes middle-of-the-night creaks, squeaks and "woo-hoos," missing socks and a profusion of the domestic phenomenon commonly known as dust bunnies. Cute. Actually, they are the nose hairs of Heckle-Nubs, which feed upon toenail clippings. (You don't even want to know the truth behind nougat.)

OK, so…I've demonstrated some techniques, shared some of my nasty creations, and given you fair warning. All that's left is for you to make your own, original monstrosities. For inspiration, seek out favorite beastie hideouts—gnarled oak roots, micro-waves manufactured before 1980, Chuck E. Cheese's and the like. Just keep a supply of Gobstoppers at the ready (monsters love those things!), and you should be fine. Probably.

MEET THE MONSTER MAKERS

Twinkie Chan
CAKE MONSTER CUTE-ILITY PACK

Twinkie Chan is superduper, ginormously excited to be part of Jenny Harada's book of monstrous fun! She has been crocheting silly goodies like tiger-head tissue cozies, frog hats with dangly legs and barbecue pork-bun plushies for her friends and family since she was ten years old. She was a weird kid! She currently lives in San Francisco, California, and works on her crafty stuff full-time after ten years in the publishing biz.

Nowadays, she imagines and handmakes all kinds of fun, food-themed accessories and cozies at www. twinkiechan.com. In autumn 2009, she contributed exclusive designs to the Hello Kitty 35th Anniversary fashion show, and her work has been featured in magazines such as *Giant Robot Magazine*, *Glamour Italia* and *Nickelodeon Magazine*. Her book of quirky crochet patterns, *Twinkie Chan's Crochet Goodies for Fashion Foodies* (Andrews McMeel Publishing), will be out in autumn 2010, and her new clothing and accessory line, Yummy You! (www.yummyyouclothing. com), will be available in stores near you around the same time!

Anna Hrachovec
NOM NOM NOMSTERS

Anna Hrachovec used to spend her free time knitting scarves and hats, but she began knitting toys in 2006 and hasn't made a scarf since. Her plush characters have an interactivity and offbeat humor that sets them apart from traditional knitted toys. Most of her strangely cute designs are turned into patterns, which knitters everywhere use to make suitable toys for people of all ages. Anna's first book of knitted toy patterns, *Knitting Mochimochi* (Watson-Guptill), was published in 2010. More patterns, tutorials and a blog can be found at her Web site, www.mochimochiland.com.

When she isn't making designs for patterns, Anna also creates special toys for gallery shows. These original pieces, which have included anthropomorphic knitted factories and city blocks, have been exhibited in New York, Tokyo, San Francisco and Seattle.

Leslie Levings
WTHP THE LISP

Leslie Levings is the maker of the Beastlies—little sculpted monsters that can be found online at www.beastlies.com. Her creatures are inspired by everything from the Muppets to vinyl toy culture and were featured on www.wired.com as one of the "Ten Things You Should Have Bought at Comic-Con." She also sculpts a weekly Web-comic called *The Atrox*, which can be found at www.theatrox.com. Leslie currently lives in Los Angeles with her husband and some cats.

Moxie
CUFF WINKS

Moxie is an artist, fiber pusher and human being. Her work has been shown in galleries in Seattle, New York, Los Angeles and beyond. Moxie likes to make wool do impossible things. She lives in Seattle and enjoys conceptual art, coffee, saying inappropriate things and bringing relentless shenanigans into the life of her husband and very dear friends.

Margot Potter
THE CORKY CREW

Margot Potter has published six books with North Light on jewelry making and design. She's a designer, author, freelance writer, consultant, public speaker, actor and vocalist, video host and TV personality who creates innovative designs for major manufacturers, books and magazines and teaches popular seminars and classes at craft and jewelry industry events. She approaches everything with her signature sense of humor, boundless curiosity and copious amounts of *joie de vivre* because she feels that if it's not fun, it's simply not worth doing. She invites people to not only think outside the box, but to tear it up, repurpose it into something fabulous and stand on it to reach for the stars. She's equally comfortable at the writer's desk, in the design studio, onstage and in front of the camera.

Her latest book, *Bead Chic*, will be released by North Light Books in fall 2010.

Dave Savage
SAVAGE GOONHEADS

Monsters have been a part of Dave Savage's life since childhood. Whether it was the imaginary Flop Monsters under his bed, Count Chocula in his cereal bowl or Sid and Marty Krofft's *Sigmund and the Sea Monsters* on TV, fun and creepy monsters were in his life to stay. At the age of six, a plastic set of fangs and a Dracula cape made by his mother were favorite playthings. In the following years he was introduced to Channel 5's Friday Fright Night, Sci-Fi Saturday and Godzilla Week. He would never be the same again.

Now Dave keeps that spirit alive with his three Web sites: http://savagemonsters.com and http://savagemonsters.mobi (devoted to monsters, robots and other cartoon creatures); and http://davesavage.net (featuring his commercial work for various clients). He has also created an iPhone application, original fonts, board games, T-shirts, buttons, stickers, posters, trading cards and way too many paper-bag puppets.

Daniel Yuhas
WOM

Daniel Yuhas is an obsessed knitter, teacher, designer and fiber artist. Check out his Web site, www.knitsybitsy.com, for the world's first knitted pillbug. Daniel's knitting designs have been published in several books and magazines, including *Interweave* and *Creative Knitting*. His fiber art has been displayed in art galleries and at mathematics conferences, and he has taught at venues ranging from fiber festivals to the local Stitch 'n Bitch he organizes in Brooklyn.

Resources

Here you'll find a few of my favorite monster-material manufacturers. Take care of your wee beasties by using the best supplies.

Suncatcher Eyes
www.suncatchereyes.net
For safety-lock eyes

Therm O Web
http://thermoweb.com
For fusible web

Swarovski
www.swarovski.com
For crystal embellishments

Duncan Enterprises
www.ilovetocreate.com
For Aleene's glue products

Polyform Products Company
http://sculpey.com
For polymer clay

Koigu Wool Designs
http://koigu.com
For fingering weight yarn

Lion Brand Yarn
http://lionbrand.com
For yarn

Beadalon
www.beadalon.com
For wire, string and beads

Index

Check out these other North Light titles.

Button and Stitch
SUPERCUTE WAYS TO USE YOUR BUTTON STASH
by Kristen Rask

Break out your button stash! In *Button and Stitch*, Kristen Rask shows you how to incorporate buttons into unique gifts, wearables and jewelry. Twenty-four one-of-a-kind projects designed by the author and a variety of talented contributors include a button bouquet, a button blossom brooch and felted buttons. Stitched items include pincushions, coasters, a fashion clutch and more. Explore creating with buttons in a fresh and fun way with *Button and Stitch*.

paperback; 8" × 8"; 144 pages
ISBN-10: 1-60061-311-X
ISBN-13: 978-1-60061-311-1
SRN: Z2913

Stray Sock Sewing
MAKING ONE-OF-A-KIND CREATURES FROM SOCKS
by Daniel

Turn your stray socks into adorable dolls! With a sock or two, thread, needles and stuffing, you can create delightful softies brimming with character. In *Stray Sock Sewing*, after reviewing sewing basics, you'll learn step-by-step how to create eight different sock creatures, from the Long-Eared Mini Doll to the Lucky Cat and the Punk Zebra. And a gallery of dozens of other sock doll creations will give you the inspiration to try your own designs as well. So gather up those socks and start creating!

paperback; 8" × 10"; 152 pages
ISBN-10: 1-60061-199-0
ISBN-13: 978-1-60061-199-5
SRN: Z2799

Stray Sock Sewing, Too
MORE SUPER-CUTE SOCK SOFTIES TO MAKE AND LOVE
by Daniel

Make friends with your socks! Every sock you have has the potential to be your new best friend with a little help from *Stray Sock Sewing, Too*. Inside, clear step-by-step instructions teach you the basics of sewing. Then you'll learn to create fourteen unique characters, including The Wise Owl, Happy Monkey and Cheshire Cat. Your socks will never be the same once you try your hand at *Stray Sock Sewing, Too!*

paperback; 8" × 10"; 144 pages
ISBN-10: 1-60061-907-X
ISBN-13: 978-1-60061-907-6
SRN: Z5760

THESE AND OTHER FINE NORTH LIGHT TITLES ARE AVAILABLE AT YOUR LOCAL CRAFT RETAILER, BOOKSTORE OR ONLINE SUPPLIER, OR VISIT OUR WEBSITE AT WWW.MYCRAFTIVITYSTORE.COM.